Elements
of
Early
Reading
Instruction

Elements
of
Early
Reading
Instruction

National Education Association
Washington, D.C.

by
R. Baird Shuman

Note

The opinions expressed in this publication should not be construed as representing the policy or position of the National Education Association. Materials published as part of the NEA Professional Studies series are intended to be discussion documents for teachers who are concerned with specialized interests of the profession.

Previously published material used in this book may use the pronoun "he" to denote an abstract individual, e.g., "the student." We have not attempted to alter this material, although we currently use "she/he" in such instances.

—NEA Publishing

Library of Congress Cataloging in Publication Data

Shuman, Robert Baird
  Elements of early reading instruction.

  (Professional studies)
  Includes bibliographical references.
  1. Reading (Elementary)—Phonetic method.   I. Title.
II. Series
LB1573.S547   372.4'1   79-10527
ISBN 0-8106-1623-8

This book is dedicated to

Raymond L. Daria,

Director of the Peaceable School Montessori

in Brooklyn, New York,

who loves kids,

who understands them,

and

who knows how to teach them.

Other books written by the author

Clifford Odets (1962)

Robert E. Sherwood (1964)

William Inge (1965)

Strategies in Teaching Reading: Secondary (1978)

The Beginning Teacher: A Practical Guide to Problem Solving (1979)
[with Robert J. Krajewski]

Edited by the author

Nine Black Poets (1968)

An Eye for an Eye by Clarence Darrow (1969)

A Galaxy of Black Writing (1970)

Creative Approaches to Teaching English: Secondary (1974)

Questions English Teachers Ask (1978)

Educational Drama for Today's Schools (1978)

CONTENTS

Preface   9

Chapter 1   A Perspective on Reading Instruction   15

Chapter 2   The Learning Processes of Young Children   20

Chapter 3   Reading Readiness   29

Chapter 4   The Basal Reader Approach   35

Chapter 5   Phonics   41

Chapter 6   Linguistic Science and Reading Instruction   48

Chapter 7   Miscue Analysis   56

Chapter 8   Dialects and Early Reading Instruction   65

Chapter 9   The Past and the Future of Reading   75

Footnotes and References   79

The Author

R. Baird Shuman is Professor of English and Director of English Education at the University of Illinois at Urbana-Champaign.

The Consultants

The following educators have reviewed the manuscript and provided helpful comments and suggestions:

Dr. Janet R. Binkley, Journals Editor, International Reading Association, Newark, Delaware

Dr. Ruth S. Smith, classroom teacher, Elm City Elementary School, Elm City, North Carolina

Carolyn S. Winningham, fifth and sixth grade Reading teacher, Pickett County Elementary School, Byrdstown, Tennessee.

PREFACE

At a teachers' workshop some years ago, I recommended to the participants a number of books on the teaching of reading which I thought might be of practical and immediate use to those in attendance. It was an after-school workshop during the middle of May. The associate superintendent of schools in charge of curriculum had made it clear to teachers that their attendance was not optional—after all, I was being paid as much as a minor league baseball player with promise might be expected to receive for two hours work, which was the amount of time I was expected to fill.

Not surprisingly, a disgruntled teacher who suffered from the handicap of professional honesty said, "I don't want to read any more books about how to teach reading. I have read too many already. I want to know what to do with kids who aren't learning, and I haven't found any book that can tell me that."

I countered, "Why do you think the books that you have read in this field are of no help to you?"

"Because they are all written by professors!" she responded.

The audience gasped. I was their guest. They were civilized people. I am a professor. People were embarrassed. I did not share this embarrassment, but I thought that these tired teachers were gracious to show their embarrassment. Truth be known, they might have cheered their colleague on for expressing their own reservations.

I suppose that I was unembarrassed by this episode because I did not take it personally, and I told the assembled teachers so. I take being a professor much less seriously than I take the challenge of working with kids who have problems with literacy and who are disenchanted with school. I still go out as often as I can and teach kids in schools. I ask to be permitted to teach those who are having difficulties and those who cause problems for the school by misbehaving. Bad conduct bothers me less than apathy among students, because students who are being obnoxious are acting out their dissatisfaction rather than letting it fester within them. (Who has not heard of the quiet, well-behaved student who goes on a shooting spree and commits wholesale murder?)

When teaching kids in a middle school, a junior high school, or a senior high school, I try to teach them outside the context of their English class, where they usually have experienced failure and defeat. I prefer to teach them reading and writing skills in classes where they are experiencing success; therefore, I have spent many days teaching in such areas as shop, forestry, agriculture, home economics, and physical education. At the elementary level, I try to divorce reading and writing instruction from an English context for students with problems in these areas and to relate it to art or music or some other area of study in which most of the children find joy and satisfaction. Learning takes place best when it is focused upon some matter of intense interest to the learner.

I hope that *Elements of Early Reading Instruction* and my earlier book *Strategies in Teaching Reading: Secondary* (Washington, D.C.: National Education Association, 1978) can be read profitably by teachers at both the elementary and secondary school levels. Regardless of level, many problems associated with reading instruction crosscut age and maturity designations. Some students in eighth, ninth, or tenth grade are, in a very real sense, beginning readers. Some preschool children are, by any definition, competent readers.

No single book or combination of books is going to provide teachers with a foolproof means of teaching reading to the broadly diverse school populations which most of them face every day. Books on reading can, however, provide teachers with insights, contexts, and reports of reliable research efforts in the field. Such information can help all teachers to proceed more intelligently in their reading instruction. Even the best teacher will still experience some failures—and the better the teacher, the more terrible these failures will seem to him or her. Teachers are the only professionals I know who feel that they have failed if they perform at less than the 100 percent level and have less than 100 percent results in learning outcomes. This reaction is what makes it exciting for me to work with teachers. They are dedicated in the healthiest sense of the word.

Elements of Early Reading Instruction has purposely been kept quite small because the writer knows that most teachers have a limited time remaining after they have fulfilled their primary professional responsibilities—teaching, preparing lessons, evaluating student work—to do much reading on their own. In the book I have tried to deal clearly and succinctly with those areas of early reading instruction which seem to me to be of the most immediate use to teachers. The second half of the book—chapters 5 through 8—will be more demanding for most readers than the first half, because it is dependent upon linguistic theory, an area in which many teachers have had little or no training. However, each of the chapters involving linguistic theory has been written so that the material should be understandable to anyone whose background in linguistic science is meager.

Most of the chapters deal with topics which have become quite controversial among those who teach reading. The second chapter of the book, which deals with the learning processes of young children, attempts to present a balanced view; however, so much data is still lacking regarding learning theory, that this chapter could conceivably be outdated before it appears in print. For example, recent research in hemisphericity may soon suggest drastic changes in teaching methodology, and a greater understanding of the brain's chemistry opens a whole new area of learning theory to those interested in the quest for more effective ways in which to teach.

The question of reading readiness, dealt with in chapter 3, remains highly controversial. We have long realized that many children can be taught to read quite early. John Stuart Mill read Greek at the age of three! But the question that must be asked is "Does early reading instruction have long-term benefits for students?" Tentative answers to that question, based on solid research, indicate that probably it is best not to push children into reading too early, even though some of them might be capable of learning the skill as preschoolers or as kindergarten students.

Long the subject of much debate, basal readers exist in so many varieties that one cannot hope to deal with them all in one limited chapter. The pros and cons are presented in chapter 4, however, as fairly as possible. Certainly basal readers are useful in some situations because they work systematically toward helping the student to develop a good sight vocabulary. Those who object to them often cite the fact that they project an image of life and a standard of living which are alien to the lives and backgrounds of large numbers of today's students.

Phonics, the subject of chapter 5, has been such a hotly debated topic that much of Jeanne Chall's landmark book *Learning to Read: The Great Debate* (1967) had to do with this single area of reading instruction. Now, more than a decade later, the great debate about phonics still continues. Teacher attitudes about phonics will likely be influenced at least in part by their definition of reading. If teachers feel that reading has been accomplished when students can decode and sound out the words written on a page, even though they may not understand what they have read—a common definition of reading among primary school teachers, who have good historical precedents for such a definition—then they may favor a strictly phonics approach to early reading instruction.

Perhaps no single force has more altered professional perceptions about reading instruction in the last quarter of a century than linguistic science. Modern linguists, particularly Bloomfield, Jesperson, Kurath, Fries, McDavid, Chomsky, and Mellon, have provided new ways to look at language and have broadened enormously the range of possibilities for teaching every aspect of the language arts. One can categorically say that a college professor of reading who has not had substantial background work in linguistic science is more a liability than an asset to his/her students. The day of the narrowly trained Ph.D. or Ed.D. in reading is virtually at an end, for which we may all rejoice.

Chapter 6 attempts to present some of the rationales for teaching reading from the standpoint of modern linguistic science. While the early attempts of Bloomfield and Fries are somewhat flawed, the emphases initiated by them are uniquely important to modern theories of reading instruction, which, at every level, reflect the lessons of modern linguistics.

Out of the transformational school of grammar founded in the late 1950s by Noam Chomsky came the impetus toward miscue analysis, a method of diagnosing reading problems through understanding and categorizing the types of reading errors (miscues) that people make in oral reading. Kenneth and Yetta Goodman led the way into this important and fertile area of study, applying linguistic theory in order to arrive at their method. Since linguists view language as a phenomenon which essentially has no more to do with right and wrong than the laws of physics have, they do not speak of language phenomena as being "correct" or "incorrect," although they acknowledge that a particular usage may be appropriate to one situation or setting and inappropriate to another. In this kind of linguistic spirit, the Goodmans prefer to speak of reading errors as miscues, thereby avoiding the negative connotation of the word "error." Indeed, to the reading teacher, miscues are not so much errors as they are indications of types of reading behaviors, and these indications can be used effectively to diagnose and remedy many reading problems.

Perhaps no question related to reading instruction is so fraught with emotional overtones as that concerning dialects. The National Council of Teachers of English has passed a resolution affirming students' rights to their own language, a right which hardly had to be affirmed by a formal resolution, because the very act of speaking is a palpable manifestation of one's right to use one's dialect. The Education Study Center, arguing that students would have greater success in initial reading instruction if their first readers were in dialect, produced three dialect readers which were received quite negatively by the Black communities for which they were designed. Subsequent research suggests that dialect readers are not particularly useful in presenting early reading instruction to speakers of dialect. What is important for teachers to realize is that dialects are regular and systematic in their forms. They are legitimate languages. In some instances they are more logical than the so-called Standard dialect. For example, the Standard "I was, you were, he was" is irregular, whereas the dialectal "I was, you was, he was" is not. The Standard "three brothers" contains a double plural (*three* and *-s*), whereas the dialectal "three brother" avoids this duplication.

12

In dealing with students whose dialects are far from the norm, teachers who wish to teach these students to read must know something about such dialects. They must, in effect, make for themselves a grammar of the dialects most frequently encountered in their schools if for no other reason than to perceive whether their students' miscues are actual misreadings or translations from the language encoded on the page into the dialect.

Teaching kids to read is probably the most rewarding pursuit in all of education. I still take more pride in helping a kid to decode something that he or she has been unable to read than I do in seeing my students finish their doctoral dissertations. The effective teacher of reading need not be a genius and need not know every theory that has been advanced in the field, although the theoretical base is important to any teacher. Rather, the effective teacher of reading must first be sensitive to people—particularly to young people—must then be caring, must then be enthusiastic, must then be patient, must then be encouraging, and must then be generous with praise.

The author owes debts of deep gratitude to many for their assistance as this book was being formed. As always, my debt to the members of the Division of Languages of the North Carolina Department of Public Instruction is great. Denny T. Wolfe, Jr., Director of the Division, is always a valued and incisive critic of my thinking and writing; Mary Sexton and C. C. Lipscomb also provided help along the way. Had the North Carolina Department of Public Instruction not provided me with the opportunity to present teacher workshops in reading all over the state, it is doubtful that I would have considered writing a book of this sort.

I was able to watch at first hand the reading and general language development of a number of preprimary, primary, and elementary school children during the years in which this book was forming. I am especially indebted to the following children and to their parents, who are cited parenthetically and who often provided food, drink, and encouragement while I was watching their youngsters grow: Khalid Abdelrasoul (Omer and Brenda) of Dammam, Saudi Arabia; Paula and Chip Reising (Bob and Nell) of Lumberton, North Carolina; Ashley Elizabeth Wolfe (Denny and Celia) of Raleigh, North Carolina; Jason, Damon, and Lluvia Anne Mendoza (Frank and Robbie) of Banner Elk, North Carolina; Cindy, Susan, and Scott Heath (Deak and Jane) of Banner Elk, North Carolina; Taimur and Kamran Sullivan (Ed and Zoreh) of Champaign, Illinois. I have observed and worked with hundreds of other children as well in schools and in reading clinics; all have my gratitude, as do the administrators who allowed me access to them.

My colleagues in the Department of English of the University of Illinois provide continuing support and encouragement, as do my administrators in the School of Humanities and the College of Liberal Arts and Sciences. Other colleagues in the College of Eduation and at the University High School have stood ready to help whenever I needed their assistance or advice. The staff at the National Council of Teachers of English have always made their library available to me when the need arose.

The staff of the University of Illinois Libraries have also been of great help, particularly Melissa Cain of the English Library who has often ordered items which I needed, and George Jaramillo of the Education Library who has responded quickly and efficiently to my requests. Florence Blakely of the Duke University Library has also gone far out of her way and has exceeded the call of duty in accommodating my requests for help.

Lucy Davis of Duke University has long been supportive and helpful. William Palmer and R. Sterling Hennis, both of the School of Education of the University of North Carolina at Chapel Hill, have provided me with insights into the reading process, as have James Cunningham of the same institution and his wife Patricia of Wake Forest University. Hathia Hayes, formerly of the North Carolina Department of Public Instruction and more recently of the University of North Carolina at Wilmington, helped to encourage my early interest in reading instruction.

I must commend three secretaries who have worked on preparing the typescript of this book. My own secretary, Eileen Posluszny, did the bulk of the typing, but when she had more work than she could handle, Katie Wood and Marlyn Ehlers gave their uncomplaining and highly efficient assistance. I am grateful to the three of them.

My aunt, Ruth E. Shuman, for over forty years a teacher in Paterson, New Jersey's School Number 9, interested me in teaching when I was a small child and helped me to see that the teaching profession is an interesting and worthy one. For this and for her interest and encouragement through the years, I am grateful.

Finally, my students in teacher training programs at Duke University and at the University of Illinois, Urbana-Champaign, have continually challenged me with new ideas which have caused me to think through many problems dealt with in *Elements of Early Reading Instruction*, as have our University Associates in Rhetoric, Joseph Berger, Joseph Bowman, Phyllis Goodman, and Thomas della Sala. Students at King Faisal University in Dammam and Al-Hasa, Saudi Arabia, where I served as Visiting Professor of English for a brief period in 1978, helped to make me aware of some of the unique problems which face non-native speakers as they strive to achieve literacy in a foreign tongue. I am deeply grateful to those who arranged for me to teach in Saudi Arabia, most particularly to Dr. Omer M. Abdelrasoul, Director of the English Program; Dr. Khalid al Saif, Vice-Rector; and Dr. Mohammed S. Kahtani, Rector of this emerging university.

Chapter 1
A PERSPECTIVE ON READING INSTRUCTION

Reading: Toward a Definition

No single, universal definition of reading, accurate and usable at all times and for all situations, has yet been advanced. The person in the street, if asked what reading is, would probably say something like "You know, it's with a book, like when you read it." Such a definition is really a nondefinition because it is circular and inexact. More sophisticated people, those who have given some thought to the matter, would arrive at a more exact definition, but they would, nevertheless, find the term difficult to define in any comprehensive way. Those who have considered it might note that we *read* people's facial expressions or that an airline pilot might respond to a controller who has just communicated with him/her verbally, "Yes, I *read* you."

We all know that reading has occurred when people give sound to symbols—words or notes of music, for example—and produce utterances:

sound

SYMBOL ————————————————————→ UTTERANCE
[word or note of music]   [or musical passage]

This is a limited form of reading, however. Someone might achieve this level of reading by producing the sounds, "John went away for two reasons: he was bored with his job and he didn't want to marry Myrtle." If, after reading this sentence, the reader is asked, "Why did John go away?" and the answer is "I don't know," some people would say that the reader has not read the passage. Others would say that indeed the reader had *read* the passage but had not comprehended it.

If you do not know German, which is a quite phonetic language, you can give utterance to (by some definitions, you can *read*) *"Ich liebe dich,"* even though you may not know what it means. Hence, in a limited way, giving utterance to symbols is reading, but it is reading narrowly defined. Such reading can be useful in some situations. If you called home and were told by your young sister that you had a postcard from Germany written in German, you might say, "Read it to me." If your sister were able to read *"Ich liebe dich"* and the name signed beneath this revealing statement, even though she had not understood the message, she would have conveyed it to you.

In hearing and understanding the message, you could use your sister's limited reading ability in German to bring you to the next level of reading ability, that of comprehension. But in this situation, you probably would not be identified as the reader; your sister would be. On the other hand, had you yourself read the post-card's message, *"Ich liebe dich,"* and known that someone was saying "I love you," you would be reading at a level one step beyond that achieved by your sister.

sound   thought
SYMBOL —————————→ UTTERANCE —————————→ MEANING

In this diagram, sound and thought may be virtually simultaneous, in which case utterance and meaning may also coincide:

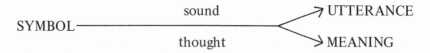

The Great Debate

The great debate of which Jeanne Chall writes extensively in her landmark volume *Learning to Read: The Great Debate*[1] is partially a debate between those who would stress phonics in reading (thereby enabling students to read *"Ich liebe dich"* without necessarily knowing what it means) and those who would stress comprehension (to the extent of saying that merely to utter the words *"Ich liebe dich"* after having seen them on a page is not a legitimate form of reading).

To those who have thought little about it—and especially to those who have long been able to read easily with good comprehension—the debate may seem inconsequential and silly. However, teachers' leanings in this debate will very much affect the way in which they approach the teaching of reading with primary school students who cannot read. The debate is therefore one of considerable importance and great moment.

It is doubtful that anyone who supports the phonics approach to early reading instruction would deny the importance of comprehension. Such people differ from those who would stress comprehension in early reading instruction only in the matter of when comprehension should be stressed.

Perhaps at this point you are thinking, "What good does it do to read if you don't know what you have read?" It seems obvious that reading is a tool whose essential function is to unlock from symbols the meanings embodied in them. However, Nila Banton Smith, approaching the question historically in *Why Do the Schools Teach Reading as They Do?*[2] writes: "For centuries absolutely no attention was given to teaching children how to get the thought from what they read. If they had learned to 'pronounce the words' their reading achievement was supposed to have been completed. . . . No attempt was made to teach pupils to read for meanings nor to check their reading after it was done to find out how much of the content they had absorbed."

The Primary School Viewpoint

The debate about how to teach reading is more alive among primary school teachers than among most other people in the population. This is because primary school teachers are confronted with the problem of teaching reading to a diverse group of first, second, and third graders, all of whom have different backgrounds which will drastically affect their ability to cope with the printed word.

If primary school teachers can get their students to sound out letters and to combine these sounds into words, they may rightfully think they have helped their students learn how to read. Few would disagree that an important initial step has been taken when students gain the ability to sound out words. Some would argue, however, that reading accomplished in this way, devoid as it may be of comprehension, does students little good and, indeed, may help to establish bad reading habits which will make it difficult for them later on to become fast and effective readers.

The main question at this point concerns whether children should be encouraged to fix their eyes on individual letters (C-A-T or M-A-N, for example) or on word configurations (CAT or MAN) or on still larger units such as phrases or clauses. Much more will be said about this matter in a later chapter.

This question and a number of others related to it have engaged the attention of teachers of reading for years; they have also caused many notable linguists to explore the whole question of how people learn to read and of how they may best be taught to read.

Linguists and Reading Instruction

Leonard Bloomfield was instrumental in defining modern linguistic study and theory. In *Language* (1933),[3] he demanded that the study of language be more scientific and objective than it had previously been and demonstrated how such an end could be accomplished. At that point Bloomfield was concerned essentially with the spoken rather than the written language. He insisted that grammar be based upon the forms and structures found within language as it is actually used. He considered that any language at any time represents a complete system of sounds and forms existing independently of the past. Such thinking, in its day revolutionary, led the way to a whole new conception of language study and linguistic understanding. Moreover, chapter 28 of *Language,* "Applications and Outlooks," provided a linguistic framework for many scholars and teachers who sought to discover a means of using linguistics to devise more effective means of teaching reading.

In 1942, Bloomfield published his much cited essay "Linguistics and Reading."[4] As early as 1937, however, he had given considerable attention to the teaching of reading, largely because he was concerned with how his own young son was learning to read. Bloomfield told the noted lexicographer Clarence Barnhart that he had devised a system of reading instruction for his own son "because the methods used in the schools were non-scientific in nature and ignored the fundamental principles of scientific study of language developed during the last 150 years."[5] Barnhart contends, "Bloomfield's system of teaching reading is a linguistic system. Essentially, a linguistic system of teaching reading separates the problem of the study of word-form from the study of word-meaning."[6] More will be said later of Bloomfield's approach to reading instruction. It is sufficient at this point to note that in the initial stages it focused essentially on acquainting students with the *phonemes* or elemental sounds of the language and on teaching them how to combine these phonemes into meaningful utterances (*man, pat, pin,* for example) or into utterances which have no meaning (*mip, nib, pos,* for example) but which are, nevertheless, pronounceable.

Bloomfield postulated that "in order to read alphabetic writing one must have an ingrained habit of producing the phonemes of one's language when one sees the written marks which conventionally represent these phonemes. . . . The accomplished reader of English, then, has an overpracticed and ingrained habit of uttering one phoneme of the English language when he sees the letter *p,* another phoneme when he sees the letter *i,* another when he sees the letter *n,"*[7] etc.

Charles Fries, writing almost two decades after Bloomfield, asserts that "One can 'read' insofar as he can respond to the language signals represented by patterns of graphic shapes as fully as he has learned to respond to the same language signals of his code represented by patterns of auditory shapes."[8] He warns that "contrary to the belief of many, *written material contains less of the language signals than does talk."9* Fries is concerned with having readers respond to units larger than phonemes, and he considers reading to have occurred only when comprehension has occurred: "Real reading is *productive reading*—an active responding to all the sets of signals represented in the graphic patterns as they build up, *and the carrying forward of such a complete cumulative comprehension as makes it possible to fill in the intonation sequences, the special stresses, and the grouping pauses that the written text requires to fill out its full range of signals."10* Clearly, he does not consider the expressionless sounding of words to constitute reading in any real sense.

Fries gleaned complexities in reading instruction which eluded Bloomfield, as excellent and indispensable as his pioneering work was. He addresses one of these complexities in the introduction to *Linguistics and Reading:* "One can learn such words as MAN, MAT, MEN, MET, the phonics way and project similar letter-sound correspondences through a substantial number of words. But even for the three letter words like MAN it is not the single letter A that indicates the vowel sound. . . . It is the spelling-pattern MAN in contrast with the spelling-patterns MANE and MEAN that signals the different vowel phonemes that identify these three different word-patterns /maen/ /men/ /min/; or MAT /maet/–MATE /met/–MEAT /mit/."11

Fries is making quite sophisticated differentiations, and comprehension is obviously an underlying ingredient in all of them. So it is in much of the work of most of the notable psycholinguistically oriented writers in the field—Frank Smith, Kenneth Goodman, Yetta Goodman, and Paul Kolers. Another member of this group, George Miller, points out, "The pen in 'fountain pen' and the pen in 'play pen' are very different pens, even though they are phonologically and orthographically identical. The words in a sentence interact."12 Comprehension is indisputably a necessary component of the interaction to which Miller alludes.

Prominent Concerns in Reading Instruction

Reading teachers have long been concerned with matters related to word attack, vocabulary building, word study (prefixes, suffixes, derivational roots, etc.), study skills, reading in specialized or content areas, oral reading efficiency, pronunciation, spelling, and the speed and accuracy with which students read. These concerns continue down to the present time, but the advent and growth of linguistic science has shed new light on the understanding of many of them.

As teachers of reading came to understand more about human psychology, particularly about the psychology of young children, the question of reading readiness became a prominent concern, and has remained one down to the present. Of all the reading researchers who warn against pushing children into reading experiences too early, perhaps none have stronger objections to using such materials as basal readers at the kindergarten level than Miles Tinker and Constance McCullough. They remind kindergarten teachers that research clearly indicates "that a half year or year later [after kindergarten] a child can learn the same things faster."13

Largely through the research of socio- and psycholinguists, attention has lately been focused upon two extremely important areas of reading instruction, *miscue analysis* and *dialectology,* as they relate to reading achievement. Kenneth and Yetta Goodman were the pioneering investigators in the area of miscue analysis; and such researchers in language as Kenneth R. Johnson, Roger Shuy, Ralph Fasold, Joan Baratz, William Stewart, William Labov, and Jane Torrey have shed considerable light upon the relationship between dialects and reading ability.

Unquestionably, a new era in the understanding of language occurred with the publication in 1957 of Noam Chomsky's *Syntactic Structures,* a book which marked the rise of transformational-generative grammar, a system with which some reading researchers had, in one way or another, been dealing earlier. A year before the publication of Chomsky's landmark work, William S. Gray wrote of sentence analysis and transforming, using the model sentence "The water in our village well is good to drink" and analyzing it as follows:

> As one reads the first two words in this sentence various associations are aroused. This grasp of meanings is restricted and made more definite as the third, fourth, fifth, and sixth words are recognized. The thoughts then retained are held in mind, as the reader continues to the end of the sentence. When he recognizes the words, "good to drink," the meaning already acquired is greatly expanded and clarified. The final idea is the result of the fusion of the meanings of the separate words into a coherent whole.*[14]*

Gray then goes on to note that the simple shifting of the verb "is" to the beginning of the sentence leads to the interrogatory transformation. Early attuned to much of the linguistic questioning and investigation going on in the 1950s, Gray was quick to see the implications of linguistic science, particularly of the transformational-generative approach to language study, for reading instruction.

Hemisphericity and the Learning Process

Despite the great advances made in learning theory in recent years, relatively little is known in any detailed way about how people learn. Promising research has been done of late in an attempt to understand more fully the workings of the brain's right hemisphere, that hemisphere which has to do with intuition and with nonlinear thinking. No wholly conclusive results are yet available, nor are they likely to be in the foreseeable future. Nevertheless, it is apparent that only a small portion of the brain's potential has been tapped and that modern schools teach to the left rather than to the right hemisphere.

The prestigious National Society for the Study of Education devoted one of its two 1978 Yearbooks to an investigation of how the brain operates and what this portends for the whole educative process. *Education and the Brain*[15] is an important book. Of considerable interest in this area also are Robert E. Ornstein's *The Psychology of Consciousness*[16] and *The Nature of Human Consciousness,*[17] Jerome Bruner's *The Process of Education,*[18] Robert Samples and Robert Wohlford's *Opening,*[19] Robert Persig's *Zen and the Art of Motorcycle Maintenance,*[20] and Robert Samples's *The Metaphoric Mind.*[21]

Certainly it is now a quite well-accepted theory that reflection has a great deal to do with learning and that the mind, once it absorbs a bit of information, no matter how inconsequential it may seem, retains that information at a subconscious or unconscious level, if not at a conscious one. As more becomes known about how to activate the mind's amazing retentive powers and to bring required information into the conscious sphere when it is needed, teaching and learning techniques will change drastically.

Chapter 2

THE LEARNING PROCESSES OF YOUNG CHILDREN

Most formal teaching is done by imitation rather than by any scientific design. We teach as we were taught. It seems safe to teach this way. Communities will accept without question the endless grammatical drill, the recitation of multiplication tables, and other exercises such as these which have characterized the educations of the people in the power structure of any advanced society. Methodology is questioned only when it departs significantly from what was done when those who control education were in school.

If medicine had been subjected to the public pressures that have normally been exerted upon education, in all likelihood we would still be treating people by routinely bleeding them, and the average person would not live to be fifty. Schools change slowly, and even when valid and compelling research data are available to educators, their effects typically are slow to be felt in many schools.

Classification of Early Learning Processes

Many classifications can be made of the learning processes of young children. A strict chronological classification, while extremely generalized in nature and rife with exceptions, can be of some help to parents and teachers. Frances Ilg arrived at a taxonomy which has been found useful. After tracing the events in children's development which lead up to reading readiness, she associates each of these events with a typical age at which it might be expected to occur. For example, between two and two and a half years of age, children are generally interested in tiny things, including "a tiny edition of Kate Greenaway or Peter Rabbit."[1] This positive feeling about one or more books, even though it may have little or nothing to do with the physical act of reading as such, is a first step toward the acceptance of books. Between two and three, children may have developed a sustained interest in stories which are told or read to them; between three and three and a half, they may have memorized stories or nursery rhymes. In reading favorite stories to children of the latter age group, it is interesting to change one key word (for example, to substitute "bird" for "butterfly") to see whether the child notices the substitution and suggests the correction.

Ilg comments that the young child who is frequently read to begins to build up a store of sight words, often based on the word's initial letter and on the memory of a story. She speculates that between five and a half and six the child "can read the word *Washington* as easily as *Jane* if the story is about Washington and he can recognize this word because it begins with *W*. . . ."[2] Among other useful generalizations that Ilg makes are the following:

- The typical first grader approaches reading with zest and enthusiasm, but will likely have trouble keeping his or her place because of the instability of the visual mechanism at that age.

- Youngsters at six may insert words, especially adjectives, into what they are reading aloud, particularly adjectives they have just read because at that age they love repetition.

- Such youngsters begin with enthusiasm, but their interest may flag because they cannot sustain it for long.

- They become mechanical readers as they approach age seven, reading in a virtual monotone, presumably because they are now becoming increasingly concerned with comprehension which may be decreased if they stop to labor over every word.[3]

Ilg's findings, based largely upon accurate observation of large numbers of children, were little influenced by the findings of neurophysiologists, much of whose most important work became available after Ilg had enunciated her conclusions about child development. The same might be said of many of Piaget's findings which also made important generalizations about the way in which children develop intellectually and physically.

Some Neurophysiological Findings

Exciting and extensive work is currently being carried out in neurophysiology with conclusions of enormous significance for education. In many instances, the neurophysiological findings support the earlier speculations and empirical findings of such seminal thinkers as Piaget, Vygotsky, Chomsky, and—much earlier—Montessori, Whitehead, and even Aristotle. It is perhaps worth noting that Montessori was a physician, so that her approach to learning and teaching methodologies was often based on strong biological evidence as well as upon philosophical and pedagogical speculation.

Epstein has recently chronicled the brain's physical growth, noting that "human brain growth occurs primarily during the age intervals of three to ten months and from two to four, six to eight, ten to twelve or thirteen, and fourteen to sixteen or seventeen years, and . . . these stages correlate well in timing with stages in mental growth."[4] It is interesting to note, as Epstein does, that all stages of growth in the brain correspond almost exactly—except for the last stage, fourteen to sixteen or seventeen—to the classical stages of intellectual development identified by Piaget.

If Epstein's research has validity, as it appears to have, then teachers should take careful note, for it indicates that periods exist when intellectual effort will yield more significant results than an equivalent amount of intellectual effort might yield at some other time. Also, as will be seen, to begin intellectual training prematurely may yield long-term negative results so that the early starter may ultimately become the student who falls behind.

Epstein's (and Piaget's) third stage is a crucial one at which initial reading instruction is emphasized. It is during this stage that most children learn to read. Although some notable experts in the field have suggested beginning reading instruction earlier than first grade, as noted in the following chapter on reading readiness, Epstein's findings would tend to discourage such early instruction. Two notable studies have revealed that learning is best achieved if students are not pushed into it too early.

Hampleman studied two groups of children, the first consisting of students who were no older than six years and three months when they entered school and the second consisting of students who were six years and four months or older when they entered school. The overall intelligence of each group was essentially the same. By the end of sixth grade, the group of students who had entered school at a later age (the older group) was approximately one-third of a year advanced over the younger group. The difference, while not statistically significant, is certainly suggestive.[5]

Of greater statistical significance were the findings of L. B. Carter who compared two groups of fifty children each, the first of which had entered school before age six and the second of which entered school after age six. Again, the groups were intellectually similar and the balance of boys to girls was controlled. The results of the Carter study revealed that by the end of sixth grade a full 87 percent of the children who entered school prior to age six had not equalled the scholastic achievement of the group whose members entered school after age six.[6] These findings are particularly suggestive when viewed in the light of Epstein's findings about the physiological stages of the brain's development.

Although some researchers have found it possible to teach reading to first graders with a mental age of less than six years, the evidence speaks merely of teaching students to do something—in this case to read—but fails to take into account the long-term benefits of doing so, as the Hampleman and Carter studies have done. Albert Harris acknowledges that it is possible to teach children of mental ages below six to read; but in seeking to do so, he warns, one must expect that progress will be slower, teacher effort greater, and the need for individualization considerably more than when working with children whose mental development is further along.[7]

As early as 1923, E. L. Thorndike, concerned with the question of readiness in relation to the physiology of the brain, discussed the behavior of neurones and their possible effects upon intellectual achievement at various developmental stages.[8] Arnold Gesell was also concerned with the question of humankind's possible developmental stages physiologically and their implications for education.[9]

Some Conflicting Views

The next chapter notes that some highly respected figures in the field of reading call for earlier beginnings in reading instruction for some children. Notable among the authorities cited is Dolores Durkin who has long had an interest in and a concern with this matter.[10] Durkin does not advocate pushing children prematurely into reading, but she feels that some children have the desire to read early and that reading instruction would not be harmful to them. Their desire is easily noticeable. They are children who love to be read to, who develop a good store of sight words, who have an interest in printed signs and in other printed objects. These children generally come from environments in which books have been important. They are generally middle- or upper-class children. But even these children, it must be remembered, may not in all cases possess the visual stability to be able to read well in any sustained way, so there is no cause to worry if they are not amenable to early reading instruction.

The frantic abandonment and disparagement of progressive education in the period immediately following Sputnik's launching in 1957 caused many influential educators to push toward the development of learning modalities which would enable students to learn things earlier. Influential among the books of the time was Jerome S. Bruner's *The Process of Education,* which enunciated rather startlingly, "We begin with the hypothesis that any subject can be taught effectively in some intellectually honest form to any child at any stage of development."[11] One must remember that this statement was presented as a hypothesis to be tested rather than, as many took it to be, a statement of Bruner's theory of education. But, because this fact was not fully realized, some educators thought that the ages of children or the stages of their development had less to do with their learning processes (including learning how to read) than did the organization of the material to be taught.

Perhaps the most interesting and carefully considered approach to early reading instruction comes from Lawrence Kohlberg, who, while not denying the mental growth that occurs between ages six and eight, feels that early reading instruction might reasonably be undertaken earlier. He writes, "A good deal of learning to read and to write in the elementary school is a tedious task for the six to eight year old, requiring drill, repetition, self-correction and considerable insecurity in comparing the child's own performance with that of other children in the classroom." Kohlberg then goes on to suggest, "Because reading and writing (especially reading) are relatively low level sensorimotor skills, there is nothing in the cognitive structure of the reading task which involves any high challenge to the older child. In contrast, the identification of letters and words can be challenging fun for younger children."[12]

One cannot easily deny the validity of Kohlberg's statement *for some children.* However, the physical development of the individual child, as well as the environmental factors which impinge on his or her learning readiness will inevitably dictate that some children cannot begin to read early and profit from doing so. Indeed, by attempting to read before they are ready, their first formal learning experience may be a frustrating one, and it is sometimes difficult for children who associate frustration with the first formal learning tasks to make a disassociation between frustration and learning in the future. Therefore, if teachers (and/or parents) are going to err in this particular matter, less harm is likely done if they err by keeping the child longer than is necessary from formal instruction than in pushing the unready child into premature learning situations.

The Mind as Receptor

The human brain is never at rest. It is always actively involved in a variety of processes, so that even when children are engaged in such seemingly passive activities as listening to someone talk, viewing television, or being read to, complex and very active mental processes are occurring within. Teachers can help to control and shape experience; but, in the last analysis, each individual must process that experience, and each will process it in a different way. Neuroscientists have found substantial evidence "that environmental stimulation helps the 'healthy' brain develop to its optimal condition."[13] Teachers can help to provide some of the environmental stimulation alluded to here. They have less control over how students process what they receive than they have in making sure that students receive some stimulation.

In line with recent discoveries about the brain and its workings, Robert M. Gagné writes that many changes have taken place in the conception of how people learn and of what learning is. He notes, ". . . investigators are shifting from what may be called a *connectionist* view of learning to an *information processing* view. From an older view which held that learning is a matter of establishing *connections* between stimuli and responses," he continues, "we are moving rapidly to acceptance of a view that stimuli are processed in quite a number of different ways by the human central nervous system, and that understanding learning is a matter of figuring out how these various processes operate." Gagné acknowledges, "Connecting one neural event with another may still be that most basic component of these processes, but their varied nature makes connection itself too simple a model for learning and remembering."[14] This statement is, of course, provocative in view of much that has been written by Jerome Bruner,[15] Benjamin Bloom,[16] and other learning theorists.

Whether learning to read is regarded as a passive or an active learning experience—and cases have been made for both views—it can never be said convincingly that the mind is not involved actively in the learning process. David Russell asserts, "The act of reading has usually been regarded as a receptive process rather than a creative one. There seems to be some justification, however, for the use of the term 'creative reading' to signify behavior which goes beyond word identification or understanding of literal meaning to the reader's interpretation of the printed materials."[17] In this statement Russell is striving to relate reading to his six major categories of thinking behavior—perceptual thinking, associative thinking, concept formation, problem solving, critical thinking, and creative thinking. What he says, however, is quite in agreement with the conclusions of other researchers about the kind of process involved in learning to read—particularly the conclusions of those researchers who think that reading has not occurred if comprehension has not taken place.

Piaget was aware that "it has been shown by the study of animal behavior as well as by the study of the electrical activity of the nervous system that the organism is never passive, but presents spontaneous and global activities whose form is rhythmic."[18] Teachers need to remember that they are dealing always with sentient beings who mold all experience which reaches them into their own interpretation of that experience. The mind is a receptor, but it is by no means ever passive. It receives, it perceives, it retrieves, it translates, it transforms, it assimilates, and in the end it retains its own image of all that has been imprinted upon it.

Incremental Learning

Most teaching is based on the fact that learning is incremental. Good teaching is a partnership between teachers and learners because it is well acknowledged that the more responsibility learners assume for their learning, the more effective is the learning experience. Bloom's taxonomy and Bruner's theory of instruction are based on the incremental nature of learning. Both stress that learning must be accomplished in small, sequential steps, with the behavioral outcome of each step clearly and specifically stated in advance. For example, in beginning reading, an outcome (behavioral objective) such as "The student will learn the Roman alphabet" would be much too broad. Rather, a reasonable objective might be "The student will learn to distinguish between the lower case block letters *b* and *d* in a printed context." Behavioral outcomes are never stated in such terms as "The student will learn to appreciate..." or "The student will come to understand...," because appreciation and understanding are not measurable in specific ways. On the other hand, a teacher can show students a picture of a boy and one of a dog and ask which one begins with /b/. The answer given will be either correct or incorrect and will be a valid test of the stated objective.

Madeline Hunter, who defines learning as "any change of behavior that is not maturational or due to a temporary condition of the organism," goes on to say, "Learning is governed by laws and proceeds incrementally."[19] Few would quarrel either with Hunter's definition, which she supports very well, or with her statement about the incremental nature of learning; however, her latter statement cannot be taken at face value without considering some other theories about the incremental nature of learning, of which more will be said subsequently.

Hunter supports her second statement by saying, "Learning is incremental. Simpler learning components make up more complex learning behaviors. Therefore, we can systematically build step by step toward a complex learning. The acquisition of a more complex behavior attests to the accomplishment of the necessary component or prerequisite learnings."[20] Hunter calls for precision in the teaching process and sagely suggests, ". . . attainability by the learner within a reasonable time is another essential property of an appropriate learning objective."[21] Each of these statements by Hunter is important for teachers; however, one caveat must be borne in mind. While Hunter contends, quite reasonably and convincingly, that all learning is incremental, she nowhere states that it continuously proceeds from increment to increment *at the same rate.* Anyone reading such an implication into Hunter's statement—and such misreadings have not been uncommon—may possess a distorted view of what she is calling for. It may well be in many cases that although increment B comes logically after increment A, some students are not ready to move from one level to the next succeeding level at a particular time. Fallow periods occur in the learning sequences of human beings, and these fallow periods, which may last for a year or more, can be followed by spurts in learning potential, *if the fallow periods are handled properly.*

The Criterion of Difficulty

Albert North Whitehead, writing in 1922, made statements which fly in the face of much that later learning theorists, such as those just mentioned, came to espouse. Nevertheless, Whitehead's arguments are so cogent that they cannot well be ignored by anyone concerned with the question of how people learn. Indeed, neuroscientists are now beginning to present research evidence to support many of Whitehead's earlier contentions.

Whitehead first states, quite commonsensically, "that different subjects and modes of study should be undertaken by pupils at fitting times when they have reached the proper stage of mental development."[22] Such a statement is so patently and universally acceptable that one might ask why Whitehead would deign to make it. Indeed, taken at face value, this statement seems to be completely consistent with what Hunter and Bloom and Bruner have contended. However, when Whitehead takes the statement one step further, its content takes an unexpected turn; he urges his reader to "consider first the concept of difficulty. It is not true that the easier subjects should precede the harder. On the contrary, some of the hardest must come first because nature so dictates, and because they are essential to life."[23] He goes on to speak of the enormously difficult challenge that language acquisition, one of the most complex and confusing learning tasks known to our race, presents to society's youngest learners. He continues, "The hardest task in mathematics is the study of the elements of algebra, and yet this stage must precede the comparative simplicity of the differential calculus."[24]

The Theory of Necessary Antecedents

Whitehead is more concerned with the question of necessary antecedents in the learning process than he is with moving from simple to less simple on to complex, as Hunter delineates the process and as Bloom and Bruner both suggest. Whitehead says that a student *cannot* read *Hamlet* if a student cannot read. In terms of difficulty, learning to read perhaps presents learners with much greater challenges than does reading a specific work after they have learned to read. But the skill must be learned, regardless of difficulty, before the second act can be accomplished. Many learning theorists appear to ignore or forget this basic and quite obvious fact, and by so doing, they may cause teachers to underestimate the degree of challenge which some early elements of reading instruction present to their students.

It may be difficult, for example, for a teacher to understand why some students can identify the word *boy* or *toy* or *girl* on one page of a primer and then, five minutes later, be unable to identify the same word on another page. Teachers who are puzzled by this phenomenon should look at a page of Arabic or Chinese or Hebrew or Greek and find one symbol on the page. Then they should scan the page looking for a repetition of the symbol. It is devilishly difficult to spot such a symbol when one is unused to the language and symbol system being used, and this is just the sort of problem with which beginning readers are faced.

Alternations in Pace

Whitehead addresses the question of whether intellectual progress is continuous or, as he calls it, periodic. This argument is the basis for his title, "The Rhythm of Education." He writes, "The pupil's progress is often conceived as a uniform steady advance undifferentiated by change of type or alteration in pace; for example, a boy may be conceived as starting Latin at ten years of age and by a uniform progression steadily developing into a classical scholar at the age of eighteen or twenty."[25] Whitehead uses the word *rhythm* to convey the sense of "difference within a framework of repetition." He is convinced that learning activity, like life, is periodic.

While Whitehead is less explicit than Piaget about the ages at which various stages of development occur, there is remarkable correspondence between the two. Whitehead does specifically contend that the three years between ages twelve and fifteen represent the optimal time for a massive attack upon language and suggests that following this period, a massive attack upon science is appropriate—all in keeping with the stages of romance, precision, and generalization which he promulgates.

Research in the physiology of the brain indicates that no new brain cells are formed after the second year of life; however, ". . . the cessation [of the production of brain cells] contrasts markedly with the increase of about 35 percent in brain weight after [age two]."[26] Epstein argues, "If these modifications occur continuously during child development, then each child at any age represents a point on a continuum of development. However," he cautions "if increases are not continuous, but rather occur at discrete periods during life, then we have to think in terms of *stages* of brain development. Such brain development stages may well manifest themselves in correlated, if not causally related, stages of mental development."[27]

Epstein's data indicate that the theory that the brain's weight increases in stages rather than continuously has considerable validity, and that these stages of increase in weight occur between two and four years, six and eight, ten and twelve, and fourteen and sixteen, with some variations attributable to sex differences.[28] These stages of the brain's physical growth are well correlated, as Epstein says, with stages of mental development. Epstein suggests that "the question of what to do during the putative 'fallow' period will be answered definitively only by executing in schools (not in psychology laboratories!) some well-designed experiments aimed directly at that question."[29] The answer to that question can have a great deal to do with the whole of anyone's intellectual development. Perhaps, as Kohlberg suggests, the "relatively low level sensori-motor skills"[30] such as reading and writing would best be taught during the fallow periods so that the more intellectually interesting tasks such as comprehension can be approached when the mind is in a growth stage. But it is equally possible that the complexities, both physical and intellectual, of initial reading and writing experiences are best handled when the brain is in a growth phase. The data on this matter are sketchy and inconclusive to date.

Hemisphericity

Little can be said in the space remaining in this chapter about the important and challenging research currently being done in hemisphericity and related fields. It has long been known that the brain is bicameral and that in most people the left hemisphere governs the actions of the right side of the body and vice versa. It is now thought that in most people, the left brain controls such operations as reasoning, analyzing, speech formation, linear thinking, verbal activity, sequential patterning, and comparison and contrast. The right brain, on the other hand, is concerned with intuition, synthesis, the holistic view of things, subjectivity, and analogical processes. The left brain is alert, the right brain aware; the left brain is controlled, the right brain creative; the left brain is knowing, the right brain absorbing; the left brain is active, the right brain receptive.[31]

We know too little about how the brain processes information, but we do know that some experiments indicate that an increased knowledge of the functions of both hemispheres of the brain could drastically change the way in which initial reading instruction is offered. Roger Sperry experimented with patients whose corpus callosum had been severed, causing their right and left brains to function independently of each other. Sperry flashed on a screen for one-tenth of a second words like KEYCASE, in such a way that KEY appeared only in the left field of vision, CASE in the right. When he asked patients what word they had seen, they said CASE. But when he had them reach into a bag and pull out the item which corresponded to the word they had seen, they consistently pulled out keys—even though they could not name what they had pulled out.[32]

In a study of a Japanese patient whose left middle cerebral artery was occluded, Yamadori reports that the patient could read Japanese ideograms (Kanji) but had great difficulty reading Japanese phonograms (Kana), presumably because the latter reading depended upon the left hemisphere, while the former activity was centered in the right.[33] It has been determined by extensive research that "pictures, generated images, and instructions to image words"[34] can have a profound effect upon the retention of information presented both adults and children.

Reporting on one of his own experiments, Wittrock writes, ". . . in reading, learners are hypothesized to use individualized abstract analytical and specific contextual cognitive processes to generate meaning for the text from their memories of earlier experiences. The sentences in the text are the retrieval clues which initiate the generative processes. In one study of reading," Wittrock reports, "one familiar synonym substituted in each sentence for an unfamiliar word doubled children's comprehension of the story and sizably raised their retention of it."[35] Such information is becoming so voluminously available that it will surely have a profound effect upon the strategies of future reading instruction as well as upon the way that future beginning reading materials are composed.

Chapter 3
READING READINESS

What Is Readiness?

Definitions of readiness abound, but perhaps no more succinct and direct one exists than Ethelouise Carpenter's serviceable statement that "readiness lies somewhere between wanting to and having to."[1] Readiness is a process of becoming, a process of bringing together the vast complex of abilities and, in some cases, materials required to perform a task be it walking, talking, reading, digging a hole, baking a cake, or whitewashing a fence in Hannibal, Missouri.

Readiness is determined by so many factors that it is virtually impossible to recognize all of them. David P. Ausubel warns that "readiness can never be specified apart from relevant environmental conditions."[2] Albert J. Harris goes beyond this statement, contending that readiness is influenced significantly by intellectual development, language development, perceptual development, sociocultural factors, and personality development.[3] Ausubel appears in essential agreement with Harris when later in his study he states, "Readiness is a cumulative developmental product reflecting the influence of all prior genic effects, all prior incidental experience, and all prior learning (i.e., specific practice) on cognitive patterning and the growth of cognitive capacities, as well as the interactions among these different variables."[4] Ausubel calls readiness "the principal developmental dimension of cognitive structure."[5]

Edward W. Dolch lists five kinds of readiness that he considers necessary before a child can embark most productively on the task of reading. He indicates that children must possess physical readiness, school readiness, language readiness, interest readiness, and perceptual readiness.[6] Dolch may be correct in assuming that readiness in all these areas is prerequisite to learning to read effectively, but in pointing out the areas in which children need to be ready, he suggests obliquely the sorts of realistic problems that today's teachers have in dealing with the great diversity of students who populate typical primary grade classrooms.

The Currency of the Term

Although the term "reading readiness" came into common use in the 1920s, "the common interpretation was that readiness is the product of maturation."[7] Durkin shows clearly how the psychology of G. Stanley Hall directly influenced the conception of readiness in reading instruction, based as it was on the belief that "each individual, as he grows and develops, passes through certain stages, and these stages follow each other in an inevitable, predetermined order."[8] This mechanistic view of human development has a certain neatness and an appealing order about it; vestiges of it are found even today in Kohlberg's stages of moral development. But this does not suggest that one should merely wait for learning to happen rather than to try to direct activities toward well-defined learning ends.

Ausubel recognizes that "to equate the principles of readiness and maturation not only muddies the conceptual waters, but also makes it difficult for the school to appreciate that insufficient readiness may reflect inadequate prior learn-

30

ing on the part of the pupils because of inappropriate or inefficient instructional methods." He then warns of a prevalent danger: "Lack of maturation can then become a conveniently available scapegoat whenever children manifest insufficient readiness to learn," thereby absolving the school of responsibility.[9]

Miles Tinker and Constance McCullough, while not denying the importance of maturation in reading readiness, state that a child "is ready to read when maturation, experience plus verbal facility and adjustment are sufficient to insure that he can learn in the classroom situation." They classify the factors involved in reading readiness as follows: "(1) intelligence and socio-economic status; (2) physical factors; (3) experience and language development; and (4) personal and social adjustment."[10]

Recent writers suggest that one cannot afford to wait for maturation to occur in beginning readers. Michael and Lise Wallach warn, "Waiting for readiness to mature is hard to justify . . . if there is something one can do to facilitate acquisition of the skill in question. The social consequences of waiting are to hold down those who are disadvantaged already."[11] The Wallachs are quite in accord with Dolores Durkin who suggests that disadvantaged children need, "instead of a postponement in reading instruction, . . . an early start with it."[12] To dismiss such children with the excuse of waiting for them to mature is to deprive them of instruction in an area which can help them to become integrated more fully into the mainstream of their society.

The first book on reading readiness was M. Lucile Harrison's *Reading Readiness*,[13] followed shortly by the influential *Methods of Determining Reading Readiness.*[14] For over four decades readiness has been the subject of considerable attention from teachers of reading. Questions remain about how readiness is best determined and about what instruments are reliable for measuring it.

When Is a Child Ready?

The pat answers to the question "When is a child ready?" have not proved satisfactory. The simplest and most absolutistic answer was provided in 1931, when Mabel Morphett and Carleton Washburne of the highly respected Winnetka, Illinois, schools concluded that a child with a mental age of 6.5 was ready to read.[15] When this finding was accepted by many as the authoritative answer to a terribly complex and difficult question, all sorts of testing programs were designed to assess the mental age of children thought to be teetering on the brink of reading readiness. The Morphett-Washburne study admitted that some children with a mental age of less than six years were able to progress in reading, although their number was small. At the other end of the scale, they found that very few children with mental ages between 7.5 and 9 had difficulty learning to read.

The problem presented by this study for contemporary teachers of reading is that it was carried out in a school situation where the population was essentially homogeneous. In today's schoools, cultural diversity is so great that measurements of mental age are not altogether reliable; the instruments are weighted against nonnative speakers of English or speakers of nonstandard English. Predictively, current tests are accurate in that those who, because of cultural diversity, score low on them are often the students who have difficulty in learning to read. As measures of intellectual potential, however, the tests are generally biased and therefore not wholly reliable. The danger of such tests is that schools will misconstrue the meaning of the scores, making the presumption that students who have a mental age below 6.5 are not ready to read and should not receive instruction in doing so.

Low scores at this point can become self-fulfilling prophecies for students; early categorization can take place and the very forces which Rosenthal and others have chronicled[16] can be set loose, ever to work to the detriment of students so categorized.

Teachers of reading may well hearken to Dolores Durkin's admonition that it is not necessary that children be "ready" in all the areas which constitute readiness in order for the teacher to begin reading instruction with them. "Instead, we should be thinking in terms of readiness in the sense that one collection of abilities makes a child ready for one kind of instruction, while a somewhat different collection might make him ready to cope with another." Durkin notes that it is an all too common belief that children "must be able to do everything—and right away. Such an assumption," she reminds her readers, "needs to be replaced by one which recognizes that a child learns to read, a step at a time; and that the important readiness requirement is that he is able to learn the first step." Durkin concludes her statement with perhaps the most important reminder of all: "Fortunately, success with that first step often prepares the child to be ready for the second."[17] At this point in reading instruction, success is all important. Children who have a strong sense of having accomplished something and of having been recognized for that accomplishment will be motivated to continued accomplishment in reading, and in their minds they will associate reading with something pleasant and rewarding.

The Physical Aspects of Readiness

Classroom teachers in kindergartens and in the primary grades must be particularly observant of signs that might suggest to them that students have physical problems which might interfere with their learning, particularly with their learning to read. Remember that a child who has never seen clearly or who has never heard well is probably unaware of having any disability. In order for people to know that their vision or hearing is inadequate, they must have some standard against which to compare it. Children who have always seen objects as fuzzy outlines or heard sounds as garbled, distant vibrations are usually unaware that anyone else sees or hears differently from themselves.

Observant teachers can detect signs of problems and can seek help for students whom they suspect of being visually or auditorially handicapped. When problems of this sort are detected early, many students can have corrected vision or hearing which approaches normal. As a result, such students will obviously be better able to achieve academically.

Visually handicapped students may seem inattentive. They may work on something like a drawing for a short period and then look out the window, seemingly having lost interest in what they are doing. They may squint when they look at objects or at the chalkboard, and they may push their eyelids and eyeballs with their fingers in an attempt to sharpen the focus by altering the shape of the eyeball. Some may have physical manifestations such as tearing or redness of the eyeball or eyelids. Some may have accumulations of mucous in the corners of their eyes or on their eyelashes. They may rub their eyes a great deal and, in looking at books, they may hold them very close, very far away, or at odd angles. They may close one eye while trying to see something. All these behaviors may point to visual problems which, if unattended, would make it difficult or impossible for the child to be able to read.

Students with hearing defects may also have difficulty developing in areas related to language. Such children may talk much less than others. Like the visually handicapped, they may seem inattentive and/or unresponsive. They may turn their better ear to the speaker or cock the head or cup their hands behind their ears. Teachers suspecting that children have hearing defects should note whether they are experiencing visible discharges from either or both ears. Also, teachers might ask such children to play a radio or phonograph, paying close attention to the amount of volume such children select in order to hear what is being played.

Some schools routinely examine children for visual and auditory acuity. In schools where this policy is not in force, teachers must be vigilant to see that any handicapped students are identified and helped. Even where examinations are routinely given, teachers should report anything that might have been over-looked in the routine examination, because visual and auditory defects can not only put children far behind in the initial learning experience but can also give them a psychological disadvantage which may remain for an entire lifetime.

Variables Which Affect Readiness

Class size can have an enormous effect upon how well a child is able to read. Holmes examined the question of class size thoroughly and concluded that the younger the student, the more desirable it is to have small classes. He contended that if children are to be taught at the kindergarten level (age five or below), a student-teacher ratio of 10 to 1 is the absolute minimum. He notes that "Other things being equal, the earliest age at which a child can be taught to read is a function of the amount of time or help the teacher can give the pupil."[18] School districts are often penny-wise and pound-foolish in staffing policies. Rather than achieve the desired ratio at the kindergarten or primary level, they later employ remedial reading teachers to try to salvage the students who might have learned to read in the primary grades had more personal attention been available to them at that point in their educations.

An important social variable affecting reading instruction is that boys and girls at age six or seven are not equal in maturity. Ilg and Ames write extensively of youngsters who are of an age, both mental and chronological, to enter first grade but who lack the maturity to succeed at the tasks required of first graders. The researchers call these youngsters the "superior immatures."[19] The majority of students so designated are boys; since boys and girls normally enter school at the same chronological age, the difference in sex can have a profound impact upon the learning situation.

Jansky and de Hirsch report, "Most studies report that girls are ready to read earlier than are boys and that they retain this advantage through the lower grades."[20] They go on to cite several studies which support their contentions quite convincingly, including one study which concludes that at age six, boys are a full year behind girls in skeletal development![21]

Most experienced teachers realize the difference in the maturity of boys and girls; these differences present teaching problems to them on a continuing basis. It is generally thought that boys do not catch up to girls in terms of maturity until puberty, so that the differences last well into junior high or middle school.

One solution to the problem would be to allow girls to enter first grade at an earlier age than boys are permitted to enter. This is not a feasible solution, however, simply because boys eventually do catch up. The more obvious solution appears to be that of providing for individual differences by reducing the student-teacher ratios in the lower grades. If this solution seems economically impractical, certainly the alternatives available should seem even more so.

Testing for Readiness

Readiness tests abound. The most commonly used are the *Gates Reading Readiness Test,* the *Gates-MacGinite Reading Tests: Readiness Skills,* the *Metropolitan Achievement Test,* the *Bender Visual-Motor Gestalt Test,* the *Pintner-Cunningham Primary Mental Test,* the *Wepman Auditory Discrimination Test,* and the *Lee-Clark Reading Readiness Test.* Also in common use are the *Harrison-Stroud Reading Readiness Profiles,* the *Murphy-Durrell Reading Readiness Analysis,* the *American School Reading Readiness Test,* the *Clymer-Barrett Prereading Battery,* the *Delco Readiness Test,* the *Dominion Tests,* and the *Lippincott Reading Readiness Test.*

Albert J. Harris indicates that most readiness tests tend to be concerned with three or more of the following measures:

1. Visual perception; matching of pictures, geometrical forms, letters, and words;

2. Verbal comprehension, including vocabulary and concepts, sentence comprehension, and following directions;

3. Auditory perception, including recognizing whether whole words are the same or different, recognizing rhyming sounds, or finding words with similar initial consonant sounds;

4. Ability to identify letters of the alphabet and digits;

5. Sample lessons, in which a small number of words are taught by a specified procedure for a specified length of time, and then ability to recognize the words is tested;

6. Rating scales for teachers to rate the children on characteristics which are not tested in the objective subtests;

7. Ability to draw or to copy a drawing.[22]

It is of the utmost importance that readiness tests be introduced in an informal, game-like atmosphere. Students should not feel threatened by such tests, nor should they ever have the sense that passing and failing are their alternatives.

Starting Early

Opinions are sharply divided on how much encouragement should be given children to begin reading early. Certainly many talented children have begun reading at phenomenally early ages. Clarence Darrow, the famed attorney, reminisces, "I cannot remember when I learned to read. I seem always to have known how. I am sure that I learned my letters from the red and blue blocks that were always scattered on the floor. . . . It must be that my father gave me little chance to tarry long from one single book to another, for I remember that at a very early age, I was told again and again that John Stuart Mill began studying Greek when he was only three years old."[23] Another prodigy, Norbert Weiner, the famed mathematician who earned a doctorate before his twenty-first year, reports that he was fully able to read at the age of five and "had full liberty to roam in what was the very catholic and miscellaneous library of my father."[24]

Dolores Durking has suggested that early exposure to reading instruction might give slower students a needed head start: "Children of relatively lower intelligence especially benefit from an early start . . . . it might well [be] that slower children need contact with learning to read that is spread out over time."[25] Notable experiments in Whitby, Connecticut, and in Denver, Colorado, have demonstrated that children can be taught the physical act of reading earlier than is usually the case. The question is whether this is the most efficient long-term procedure. While much research remains to be done in the field, some early suggestive findings are in and point to the fact that too early a start may result in beginning for children a cycle of failure which impedes their future learning. Spache's much cited study[26] found that the children in the two lowest quartiles of the study whose reading program was begun in January or March scored higher on reading tests at the end of the year than comparable students who had been introduced to reading instruction in September or November.

What Teachers Can Do

Kindergarten teachers and teachers in the primary grades should not push their students into reading. Nevertheless, they should build the best reading environment possible within their classrooms. Language in all its manifestations should be used constantly—stories should be told; dramas should be enacted; books and other attractive reading materials should be abundant; posters should be displayed; items such as desks, chairs, tables, walls, windows, erasers, plants, etc., should be labeled with their names in block letters.

Teachers should note whether any students can read fluently from books around the room. Can these students read silently as well as orally? Can they recognize words from the stories they read when the words are isolated? Can they read lower case as well as upper case words when they are printed on cards? Can they differentiate among such letters as *b, d, p,* and *q*? among *h, m, n,* and *u*? among *C, D, G,* and *O*? Do they sound their vowels in such a way that there is a differentiation among *pan, pen,* and *pin*? among *tan, ten,* and *tin*?

Students should be encouraged to tell stories to the teacher, who will print these stories in block letters on sheets of paper. Students often begin reading with relative ease if it is their own stories they are reading. They also enjoy reading stories that other students in the class have told the teacher. When such stories are written (and they may be only a sentence or two in length at the beginning), the student should be encouraged to copy his or her story in block letters resembling those in which the teacher has written it.

The most important and reassuring thing that can lead to reading readiness is the natural introduction of print media of all sorts into the classroom. Such media should be introduced into game situations such as playing store in which reading labels and dealing with play money will enhance the early reading skills of young students.

The skillful teacher of young children will work to bring them to the point of wanting to read and will then carefully pilot them through the shoals to the point of their reading to satisfy needs.

Chapter 4
THE BASAL READER APPROACH

What Are Basal Readers?

Basal readers or, as they have recently been designated by some publishers, "reading systems," come in series by grade levels. They are sets of basic reading books, usually attractively illustrated, in most cases designed for use in grades one through six. Some few series run from kindergarten through grade eight. Sets of basal readers are accompanied by detailed teacher manuals and by workbooks for student use. Their chief appeals are that they are sequential and that they can be used successfully by teachers with limited backgrounds in the teaching of reading for initial instruction in that skill. Nila Banton Smith, while not blind to some of the limitations of basal readers, has noted, "Vocabulary is carefully controlled from book to book, and sequential and balanced skill development programs are provided."[1]

The basal readers used in grade one are crucial because, for most children, the first exposure to formalized reading instruction will occur at that time. The first grade series will usually contain a reading readiness workbook, a number of preprimers, a primer, and an initial reader, although some recent series have altered these traditional designations. At this level teachers are usually provided with other materials to use with students who are learning to read. The first half dozen stories in the first preprimer may be reproduced in the form of a large book, about two feet wide and three feet high, for use with the whole class. Pictures and cards containing letters, words, and phrases, along with a holder for such cards, are also a part of the typical basal reading package which schools buy for their first grades. Some packages have all sorts of supplementary reading materials for each level, along with such mediated materials as filmstrips, audio cassettes, and records related to the readings and to the reinforcement of the skills stressed in the readings. Basal readers usually give their most concentrated and continuous attention to the skills of vocabulary development, word attack, and comprehension.

Some Limitations in Basal Readers

A publishing company which decides to offer a basal reading program usually does considerable field research before embarking on an undertaking which has significant economic implications for the company. It is also careful to select highly knowledgeable reading specialists to compose and compile the books in the series. Because such books must be acceptable to large constituencies, they must generally avoid glaring controversy and must project the smiling aspects of life. Herein lies a major weakness in such books. Often they tend to be vapid, uninteresting, unrealistically optimistic, and, even in our time—despite efforts to reflect our society's great ethnic diversity—representative of the value system of white middle-class America. Efforts to bring the materials in basal readers more into the context of contemporary society have not been overwhelmingly successful.

The language of most basal readers (with the exception of the highly controversial dialect readers such as *Ollie, Friends,* and *Old Tales* produced under the direction of William Stewart by the Education Study Center in Washington, D.C.) is so-called "Network Standard," a dialect quite distant and distinct from that to which typical first graders in many of today's schools are most frequently exposed in their daily lives.

Another significant problem presents itself because such wide differences occur among the common vocabulary of basal readers. In 1960, Helen Behn examined seven commonly used preprimers and primers and reported that one-third to one-half of the vocabulary found in each was found in the others. In the same year, Walter McHugh did a similar investigation of second and third grade basal readers and found that in this group two-thirds of the vocabulary was common in all of them.[2] Obviously, while the problem moderates in the upper grades, a significant problem still existed when these studies were done. The implication of Behn's and McHugh's findings is that a school district had to commit itself to using one basal series in order not to place students at a disadvantage and expose them to a futile and frustrating reading experience. Even though these studies were conducted in 1960, more recent investigation of new basal readers reaches similar conclusions. Barnard and DeGracie, writing in 1976, reveal that in the first grade books of the eight publishers whose reading systems they investigated, ". . . a total of 1,778 different words [was] introduced in the new programs. At a specific level, about one-third of the words were common to two programs. When all words were considered across all levels [readiness and pre-primer through first reader] only 47 percent of the words were common to two or more series."[3]

But a related problem of considerably more importance, because it is outside the control of the school, is that of student mobility. American families are continually on the move; children who are exposed to one basal reading program in the first four or five months of first grade and then move to a district in which another program is used, as often happens, will all at once find it very difficult to read material which is thought to be at their grade level. Also, school districts may find themselves locked in with a costly basal reading program. If, after three or four years of using a set, districts decide that they want to adopt another reading program, they can do so only gradually because students who have gotten two or three years into one basal program cannot be easily moved into another, nor should they be.

Despite the many improvements that have been made in the basal reading systems which have appeared in the 1970s, the commonality of vocabulary is such that a child who has been exposed, for example, to the Macmillan program would have been exposed to 234 of the 510 words introduced during the first year in the Houghton Mifflin program or to 235 of the 675 words introduced in the first year of the Scott, Foresman program.[4] Rodenborn and Washburn, writing of six basal series which they examined for vocabulary, conclude that "the variations in the vocabulary introduced in these six series indicate that it will be exceedingly difficult for children to move from one series to another during or at the end of first grade."[4a] They also express dismay—quite understandably in the light of their findings—that some school districts allow multiple adoptions of basal programs.

A Lockstep Approach

Perhaps the most serious objection of educators to basal reading instruction is that it represents a lockstep method in many respects. Most people realize that children grow at different rates; that readiness comes to them at different times; that, as was noted in the preceding chapter, girls in elementary school are usually more mature than boys. Everything points to the fact that individualized instruction is the most effective type to use with beginning readers, each of whom must be encouraged to begin reading when he or she is ready to do so and each of whom must be encouraged to progress at his or her own pace which may fall behind or leap ahead of that experienced by the other students in the class.[5] The basal reader, if it is used as directed by many teachers' manuals, requires the teacher to approach each lesson according to a specific sequence:

1. Creating interest and establishing motivation;

2. Presentation and study of words new to the series;

3. Reading
   a. Directed silent reading,
   b. Rereading and oral reading;

4. Skills development and practice;

5. Follow up (usually workbook or ditto pages).[6]

Because each selection must be approached in this manner, the pace is slow and the interest level of bright students may lag. Also, slow students for whom this approach is too fast, may fall behind. The dependence on teacher direction weakens the program for students who are developing speedily. Hunt correctly asserts, "Until a fledgling reader is able to propel himself through printed material without teacher direction, he is not a reader."[7] Because of his belief in the validity of this statement, Hunt emphasizes the early need for more silent reading and for the sort of sustained silent reading of which mature readers must be capable.

Toward Individualization

Some producers of modern basal reading systems, recognizing the need for more individualization and for more flexibility within their systems, have made efforts to provide teachers with materials which will encourage a more individualized approach to reading instruction and which will allow for greater individual progress at varying rates. One program, for example, is composed of six basic units, each of which has fifty children's books covering a broad range of interest and ability levels—biographies, scientific books, adventure books, books about fantasy, and stories about boys and girls much like those who will be reading them. Each book contains several cards, each of which directs the reader to perform certain tasks related to the book, including activities concerned with vocabulary, details, comprehension, and suggestions for follow-up activities. The tendency to build individualization into basal programs in reading is promising, although in most cases it is still less refined at the lower grade levels than at the higher ones.

Increased Vocabulary

One promising aspect of some new basal programs is that they are introducing students to more extensive vocabularies as well as to more sophisticated grammatical structures. The latter phenomenon may be attributable to the fact that in the last two decades, numerous highly competent linguists have turned their attention to reading instruction. For whatever reason, while Olson's analysis of the vocabulary used in seven basal reading series at the primary level in 1965 revealed that the average number of words introduced to students during their first year of reading instruction was 324,[8] on the other hand, Barnard and DeGracie, doing a comparable study ten years later, found that the average number of new words introduced in eight of the new basal reading systems was 504.[9] This is a 66 percent increase in the number of words taught.

George and Evelyn Spache reported in 1969 that of the basal readers then in common use, the cumulative vocabulary at the end of the first reader ranged, according to the program, from 230 to 475 words.[10] Although the comparative study of six new basal readers done in 1974 by Rodenborn and Washburn[11] revealed increases in the cumulative vocabulary at the end of the first year at the lower end of the scale, the program that introduced the smallest number of new words (324) still introduced over 50 percent more words than the comparable book in the Spache investigation. But more significant is the fact that while the largest cumulative vocabulary noted in the Spache study was 475, the comparable figure in the Rodenborn/Washburn study is 675.

The Barnard/DeGracie study published in 1976 examined eight major basal programs and came up with even more encouraging data than were presented in the Rodenborn/Washburn study. Barnard and DeGracie found that the cumulative number of words introduced by the end of the first reader ranged from a low of 440 to a high of 811, with the next highest program reported on introducing 614 words.[12]

The implications of this percentage gain are in themselves important. The broader the vocabulary range of initial reading materials, the more varied they can be and the more grammatically sophisticated they can become. However, another interesting finding in the Rodenborn/Washburn report is that 51 of the 298 common words found in the six basal readers examined are not found on the Harris-Jacobson List for First Grade,[13] certainly suggesting that a broader range of relevant material is being presented in the newer basal readers than was apparent in their predecessors.

How Relevant Are Basal Readers?

Basal readers have been attacked through the years for being bland. Fred Busch writes accusingly to this point: ". . . the bland, pollyannaish content found in most first grade reading texts not only stifles the growth process, but more importantly may communicate to the child that this must be something to be frightened of and avoided. Why else would the characters not show emotion that is negative as well as positive, feel anxiety and pain, or experience conflicts?"[14] The problem which Busch addresses here is a highly complex one and it certainly has not been overcome completely. A hopeful sign of change is seen in the broadening of vocabulary used in first grade readers. Also, one cannot deny that there is some validity in Terry Johnson's statement, "The last few years have seen a marked improvement in reading programmes with regard to content. More readers deal with city children, coloured children, and children with problems." Johnson complains, though, "Literary merit is still lacking in the earliest readers,"[15] and one might also add that it is in the earlier readers that the material is still the most unrealistic and vapid.

Change does not come quickly, particularly to anything so large as a reading program. Publishers who gamble extravagantly risk losing huge sums of money and seriously jeopardizing the economic futures of their companies. Nevertheless, a sensitivity on their parts to social change is showing itself in some areas of textbook publishing.

Sex Bias in Basal Readers

Thomas R. Schnell and Judith Sweeney conducted a study, which needs to be conducted on a much broader scale than theirs, on sex role bias in basal readers and presented some disturbing conclusions. In comparing the 1966 and 1971 editions of just one major basal reading program, they found that in this program stories featuring boys had increased from 39.4 percent in 1966 to 51.2 percent in 1971, while stories featuring girls had dropped from 15.8 percent to 12.5 percent in the same period. They also found that illustrations showing boys had increased from 56.2 percent to 70.5 percent, while illustrations showing girls had dropped from 43.8 percent to 29.5 percent. All the statistics which they cite indicate that woman received less representation in the 1971 edition than in the earlier edition, and particularly that the disbalance was greater in the first grade than in other grades. It must be pointed out, however, that they examined just one series, albeit one frequently used.[16]

Another pertinent study in this area is that of Lenore J. Weitzman and Diane Rizzo[17] who in 1974 analyzed illustrations found in textbooks used in grades one through six of average U.S. classrooms over a five-year period for their latent content concerning male and female behavior. Among their findings were the following:

- Females made up only 31 percent of the total illustrations, males 69 percent. The percentage of illustrations showing females decreased from lower grades to higher grades, whereas the percentage of illustrations showing males increased.

- A strong contrast was found between the activities of boys and girls. Boys were involved in action and adventure, in outdoor pursuits; while girls were found to be passive and indoors.

- Differences in emotional expression were noted. Girls were shown expressing a wider range of emotions than boys who were shown controlling emotions—being strong and silent.

- In the reading series, among all the story titles, boys were predominant in 102 stories; girls were featured in 35 stories where they reinforced traditional female roles. Females predominated in two areas—as mean and evil characters (witches and villains) and as clumsy or stupid people or objects of jokes.

Clearly, the latent content of many textbooks deserves serious consideration.

Personal Reading Needs

Child psychologists have written voluminously to counter the notion that young children will be adversely affected by an introduction to literature which deals with problems like those they are facing in their own lives. Erik Erikson has written persuasively of children's need during the latency stage to find a means of dealing with what is going on inside them.[18] Their early literary experiences could meet this need except for the fact that parents have not yet been made fully aware of the desirability of exposing children to the sort of searching questions which might be evoked. Until a campaign to educate the public succeeds, it is doubtful that change in basal readers will be so pronounced as informed educators and psychologists would like it to be.

Chapter 5
PHONICS

What Is Phonics?

Phonics involves learning to know the relationship that exists between a sound and its graphemic representation, usually between a single letter (*b, d, t,* etc.) or a combination of letters (blends such as *bl, tr,* etc., digraphs such as *ch, sh,* etc., and diphthongs such as *oi, ou* as in *out, ow* as in *now,* etc.) and the corresponding sound which such letters may represent. Letters do not have sounds as such; they merely are a means by which commonly agreed upon graphemes represent their corresponding phonemes. People who understand these correspondences can read any word with a fair degree of accuracy even though the word is one which they have never before encountered.

As you look at this page, you can sound out the letters of *renafutopid* even though you have never seen it before and even though it is not a word in the English language (nor likely in any other language). You may not know where to accent such a word, but you can pronounce it. Having sounded it out, it will have no meaning for you because you have never before encountered it. However, if you sound out *baseball,* assuming that you had never before seen that word, you would likely make the association between the letters on the page in that specific combination and a word which is part of your oral vocabulary. From that stand-point, a knowledge and understanding of phonics can be a boon to beginning readers. Endless numbers of words can be sounded out by anyone who possesses even a limited knowledge of phonics.

What Letters Are Most Important?

Teachers do not teach phonics by working their way through the alphabet from *a* to *z*. Some letters are more efficiently and productively taught to beginning readers than others. An early decision to make is whether to teach consonants or vowels first or whether to teach them in combination. Another decision concerns whether emphasis should be placed on whole words or on parts of words, such as the initial sound and its graphemic representation. A third decision has to do with the priority in which letters are to be taught.

Normally consonants are taught before vowels. Consonants correspond more nearly to their sounds than vowels do. McKee contends that a knowledge of some commonly occurring consonants, those which usually represent just one sound in English (*b, d, f, h, j, k, l, m, n, p, r, t, v,* and *w*), will enable students to read some basic materials.[1] They will be able to do some contextual guessing and will supply vowel sounds even though they might not know their vowels by sight at this point. Such students would certainly be able to make a more successful effort at reading *Jan had Dan to her den* without knowing vowels (J-n h-d D-n t- h-r d-n) than without knowing consonants (-a- -a- -a- -o -e- -e-), although they would predictably make some miscues in reading the sentence. But the sound of each consonant gives a good clue to what is on the page.

42

The "order of primitivity" which the Institute of Logopedics of the University of Wichita developed based upon physiological data indicates that originally consonantal sounds developed in language in the following order: *m, p, b, t, d, n, h, w, f, v, k, g, th, sh, zh, ch, j, s, z, r,* and *l*.[2] Dechant states, "Experience shows that when a child suffers a speech loss, the loss is in reverse order. The last sounds to be developed are the first sounds to be lost,"[3] and most students tend to develop sounds in this order.

Clearly, the letters which should be taught first are those which have the most regular correspondences to the sounds which they represent. From this group, the letters which are most frequently used should be taught first. Letters whose names do not correspond to their sounds (notably *h* and *w*) should not be taught until children have developed a secure grounding in basic phonics. Letters which occur infrequently, particularly those which represent more than one sound (*x,* which can represent six different sounds, but which most often represents one of two sounds—*ks* or *gz*; *q,* which cannot be used in isolation and which is pronounced *kw* with the addition of *u; k,* which is fairly infrequent and is identical in sound to the *c* in *cat*; *v,* which is infrequent and which will cause children from Spanish-speaking backgrounds confusion; *y,* which sometimes has almost a consonantal value, as in *yes* and other initial positions but is a vowel in 97 percent of its occurrences, as in *day;*[4] and *z,* which is infrequently used and which has different sounds in, for example, *zebra* and *azure*),[5] should not be used or taught in the earliest stages of reading instruction.

What Is Required for Early Reading?

Even assuming that a child who is in the early stages of learning to read has already mastered the left-right, top-to-bottom directional aspects of reading English texts, the decoding process is one of the most complex challenges made of anyone in any learning situation. A study by Berdiansky and others[6] analyzed 6,092 one- and two-syllable words drawn from over 9,000 different words which they culled from the speaking and writing of a large number of children in the six-to-nine age group. Analyzing these words, they found that children, in order to learn to decode them, would have been exposed to 211 distinct and discrete phoneme/grapheme correspondences. They would have encountered situations relating to 166 rules, 60 of which relate to consonants specifically, and 69 of which are spelling pattern rules. There would be exceptions to 45 of the 166 basic rules.

Part of the reason for such complications stems from the fact that English has a borrowed alphabet, the Roman alphabet, which is suited to the phonology of the Latin language. In English, somehwere between 39 and 44 sounds (depending on which linguistic expert you read) must be represented with a basic alphabet of 26 letters. This means that some letters must represent more than one sound (like the *c* in *can* and *ceiling* or the *s* in *same* and *his*) and that certain combinations of letters must be used to make other sounds (as *ph* /f/ or *sh* /sh/, each of which is a single sound even though it is graphemically represented by two letters).

Some letters that have come to us from the Romans have no phonemes of their own in English (*c,* aforementioned; *x,* which can represent any of six different sounds; and *q,* which cannot be used alone and which in combination with *u* produces the blend /k/ /w/ and in combination with -*ue* is rendered /k/ as in *queue* or *unique* or *plaque*). Some letters are silent like the *k* in *know,* the *w* in *whole,* the *c* in *track* and the *gh* in *daughter.* Terminal *e* is generally silent in English, although it will alter the sound value of the preceding vowel, which is what differentiates *mat* from *mate* or *rot* from *rote.* But this rule is not consistent—*for* and *fore* are pronounced exactly alike.

Vowels are much more tricky to teach than consonants because they have less sound/letter relationship than consonants. The only vowel that represents only a vowel sound is *a.* For every other vowel there are exceptional usages which relate to a consonant sound: *e* in *azalea* is consonantal /y/; *u* is both consonantal /y/ (*unite*) and /w/ (*persuade*); *o* is /w/ in *choir* and *one.*[7] Terminal /e/ in English is usually rendered by *y*: *many, happily,* etc. While the experienced reader deals easily and naturally with these problem words and a host of others—particularly with such homonyms as *cite/site/sight*; *one/won; for/fore/four; ceil/seal; sail/sale; choir/quire;* and hundreds of other similarly confusing words—the beginning reader who tries to sound out such words phonically may have incredible difficulty. Teachers need to be sufficiently sensitive to their students' dialects to know whether such pairs as *talk/tock* and *daughter/dotter* are homonyms for them.

The Final E Rule

Early in their reading instruction, probably before any formal work is done specifically with long vowel sounds and with the corresponding letters, students need to know that a final *e* preceded by a consonant which is preceded by a vowel usually lengthens the sound of the preceding vowel so that, as we have noted, *mat* becomes *mate* and *rot* becomes *rote.* This is a fairly consistent rule, but it is not always operative; if it were, *come* and *comb* would have the same pronunciation. However, in *come* and *done* the *o,* rather than being sounded as a long *o,* is sounded as a short *u.*

In an early phonics approach, which is a letter-by-letter approach or, in oral reading, a sound-by-sound approach, beginning readers process a word by proceeding from left to right, sounding each letter as they go, until they produce a familiar set of consecutive sounds and know that they have read a word. The order of their reading in a word like *MAT* is a 1-2-3 order, at the end of which the word *mat* has been sounded out. However, if they are dealing with the very similarly spelled word, *MATE,* they find themselves forced, if they are to read correctly, to follow a new pattern of word attack: 1-2-3-4-2-3 or 1-2-3-4-3-2. The eye movements involved are now six rather than the three involved with *mat.* But over and above this, a new reading protocol must be advanced, so that the introduction of the final *e* rule is demanding of the students being taught it. Teachers need to appreciate the complexity of this process which for most of them is so simple and so automatic.

Vowels

Vowels present peculiar problems, largely because vowel sounds are less uniform in their phonemic/graphemic correspondences than are consonant sounds. Regional differences are more noticeable in vowel sounds than in consonant sounds. In some parts of the country, *tan, ten,* and *tin* are virtually indistinguishable from each other. Whereas Mazurkiewicz distinguishes 168 consonant graphemes (as opposed to the approximately 18 consonants found in the Roman alphabet), he identifies 265 vowel graphemes which represent a total of 16 vowel phonemes.[8] Given this complicated situation, teachers should first help their students to differentiate between short and long vowels.

Short vowels occur more frequently in English than long vowels, so probably they should be taught first. If students are guessing at the vowel sound in word attack, they are more likely to guess correctly if they give the vowel the short sound. The sound values of short vowels are as follows:

a as in *bat, attire, about*
e as in *bend, elm, help*
i as in *bin, inch, improve*
o as in *bottle, dot, rob*
u as in *uncle, study, but*

Long vowels are sounded like vowel letters in the alphabet when they are read in isolation, even though the graphemic representation may be a digraph. That is, the *ee* in *bee* and the *ea* in *sea* are pronounced identically and sound just like the letter *e* would sound if someone were reciting the alphabet. The long *a* sound may have many graphemic representations (*ai* as in *sail*, *ay* as in *pay*, *et* as in *filet*, *er* as in *dossier*, *aigh* as in *straight*, etc.), yet it is always pronounced just as the first letter of the alphabet is pronounced by someone saying the ABCs.

Students should also be introduced ultimately to the open syllable rule which decrees that when a syllable ends in a vowel sound, the vowel is long, as in *hu - mid*, or *re - cent*. When a syllable ends in a consonant sound, the vowel is short, as in *con - sent*. This rule cannot be taught before syllabification has been worked on. It is a useful rule to know, however, and it should be taught, even though it has some notable exceptions.

Irregular Spellings

In early reading instruction, as we will note in the following chapter on linguistics and the teaching of reading, it is probably best to avoid most irregularly spelled words until the students have gained considerable ability and confidence in reading words which are regularly spelled. Bloomfield adhered to this principle to the extent of excluding from his earliest lessons such words as *the, mother,* and *father*, which somewhat limited the range of sentences he could make. Perhaps some exceptions should be made, as they were in Fries's program, but these should be strictly limited.

Jack Bagford suggests, "High frequency, but irregularly sounded, words probably are more efficiently taught by a sight method while phonetically regular words and words which contain easily learned sounds probably are better taught by a phonic method."[9] Bagford calls for an eclectic approach to early reading instruction and is moderate in his tone, reminding teachers, "Phonics content is taught so that children have a tool to identify words which are known in the spoken form but not in the printed form."[10] By combining phonics and the sight word approach, beginning students can enjoy the best of two possible worlds, and early reading materials can be more varied and better related to student interest than would be possible if the phonics approach were used exclusively.

Attempts at Spelling Reform

The inadequacy of the Roman alphabet to represent fully and directly the sounds of English, which is, after all, a Germanic rather than a Romance language, has caused all sorts of inventive people from Benjamin Franklin[11] on down to the present to make attempts to reform English spelling. In the 1930s, the *Chicago Tribune* went over to reformed spelling and for years published its paper in accordance with its new spelling rules, which rendered *through* as *thru, night* as *nite,* etc.

Relatively little of such reforms reached the schools in any organized way until the 1960s when Sir James Pitman, a Briton, devised what was first called an "Augmented Roman Alphabet." This developed into what is commonly referred to as the "Initial Teaching Alphabet," often rendered merely *i. t. a.*

In Pitman's scheme, every long vowel has its own symbol, so that readers are guided to the intended pronunciation. The terminal *-s* in a word like *was* is rendered with a backward *z* ($\leq$) and the word *was* would be written *wo* $\leq$. Words like *said* and *dead* would be written *sed* and *ded* respectively. One who can read conventional English can read a text written in Pitman's system with no special training. It would seem that this variation on the Roman alphabet would yield encouraging results; however, the system was tested out extensively, and the preponderance of research data available indicate that while exposure to this system appears not to have harmed beginning readers, it did not improve their performance. Most schools have now abandoned the use of i. t. a.

The Analytical or Synthetic Approach?

Phonics can be taught analytically or synthetically. The analytical approach begins with the whole word and then breaks it down (analyzes it) into its component phonic elements. On the other hand, the synthetic approach begins with the graphemic/phonemic correspondences which students first learn and then apply by blending the sounds of the letters in words into consecutive utterances which result in a pronounceable unit (a word, unless students are dealing with nonsense syllables). Although the analytical approach is the more popular one among teachers,[12] research evidence suggests that it is less effective than the synthetic approach.

In a study conducted in Virginia, data were collected and compared for 484 first grade students, 248 of whom were taught according to the analytical approach and 236 of whom were taught according to the synthetic approach. The groups were essentially equal in age, ability, and background. The researchers report that "When the means of the synthetic program groups ... are compared with those of the analytical program groups, ... a great preponderance of differences among means (ninety-two out of 125, or 75 percent) is found to be significantly in favor of the synthetic group. In only three instances are the obtained differences in favor of the analytical group."[13] This is rather compelling research evidence in favor of the synthetic approach, and it really supports quite significantly some important conclusions reached by Jeanne Chall in *Learning to Read: The Great Debate,* in which Chall writes, "A recent study by Bleismer and Yarborough (1965), published after a major portion of this chapter was written, tends to confirm my basic interpretations of the past classroom experiments as well as my judgment that a novelty [Hawthorne] effect did not have a major influence on their results."[14]

46

The Great Debate

Perhaps the most valuable book to date to deal extensively with the subject of phonics is Jeanne Chall's. This book is carefully, indeed meticulously, researched. It has examined every significant research study in reading done during the period upon which it focuses, 1910 to 1965. Its conclusions and recommendations, objectively arrived at, cannot be ignored—although many of them have been.

Chall is clear in her statement of how initial reading should be taught if it is to be most effective: "The evidence from the experimental studies analyzed so far indicates that unselected children taught initially by a code-emphasis generally do better in reading than children taught by a meaning emphasis, at least up to early fourth grade."[15] It is evident that more research needs to be done. For example, future researchers might examine the adult reading abilities of people over twenty who were taught by the two methods. Some researchers feel that the whole word approach in the long run produces readers whose speed and comprehension are better than the speed and comprehension of people who learned to read through the synthetic phonics approach. But to date there is no hard evidence that such is the case.

With the caveats that (1) she endorses the code-emphasis approach only for *beginning* reading and (2) that she does not endorse one code-emphasis method over another, Chall announces that ". . . the research from 1912 to 1965 indicates that a code-emphasis method—i.e., one that views beginning reading as essentially different from mature reading and emphasizes learning of the printed code for the spoken language—produces better results, at least up to the point where sufficient evidence seems to be available, the end of the third grade."[16] This statement is cautious, as is most of what Chall says; but it is also clear.

The appearance of the Chall book did not mark the conclusion of the great debate; it flourishes still and research data are still coming in. More data will be required to lay to rest many of the questions which have been raised; but for the time, it seems clear that the old phonics approach of the *New England Primer* was not wholly ineffective.

Didactic and Analytical Approaches

The ever-popular McGuffey readers, while stressing meaning and requiring students to identify and memorize sight words at the beginning of each selection, used what would today be called an analytical phonics approach to some extent. That is, they taught pupils "to identify words and read sentences. . . . Having read a few lessons in this manner," they tell the teacher, "begin to use the Phonic Method, combining it with the Word Method, by first teaching the words in each lesson *as words*; then, the elementary sounds, the names of the letters, and spelling."[17] These readers, largely because of the back-to-the-basics movement, have begun to come back into vogue, but teachers should be cautioned that no research evidence exists to suggest that the approach of these readers is superior to the direct, didactic code-emphasis approach which Chall's findings indicate yield the most promising results for beginning students.

Perhaps the didactic approach is the only feasible one to use with children of five or six. Mazurkiewicz addresses the point: "Discovery-type decoding instruction, though successful in the case of many pupils, apparently has not been effective in increasing reading achievement in a large number of others since, according to Piagetian theory, the average child has not yet developed sufficient cognitive skills to allow him or her to induce the grapheme-phoneme relationships."[18] This is not to say that the primary school years are not a time of discovery; rather it suggests that in beginning reading instruction, the discovery method is inefficient. In a typical school day, the opportunity for discovery is great and skill in reading can help to promote it. But the students desperately need to gain skill in reading at this stage of development, and the great weight of reliable research cited by Chall and Mazurkiewicz, both of whom have been exhaustive in their investigations, indicates categorically that the didactic method of beginning reading instruction will lead students most effectively to the desired end.

A Final Word

Teachers of reading, particularly those involved in initial reading instruction, need to believe in what they are doing, and they must approach their task with a good knowledge base to support them in what they are doing. Some eclecticism is healthy and desirable; not all children learn best by the same method. However, teachers must be aware of the research data which are continually coming in if they are to be the kinds of informed professionals who can best work with the young child and help him or her to gain possession of that skill which the modern world values above all others, the skill of literacy.

Chapter 6
LINGUISTIC SCIENCE AND READING INSTRUCTION

Linguistics Defined

The term *linguistics* has been variously defined. The general term includes such areas as *historical linguistics,* which has to do with the historical development of language through the ages; *descriptive linguistics,* which is concerned both with speech sounds (phonology) and grammar (how language patterns are structured, which in turn involves morphology and syntax); *linguistic geography* and *dialectology,* which catalogue and describe languages as they are used in various regions and/or by various groups of people; and *comparative linguistics,* which is concerned with relationships among various languages of common origin, such as the Indo-European family of languages or, more narrowly, the Romance or Germanic languages, both of which are subdivisions of the Indo-European group. Overlaps exists within these classifications. Comparative linguistics, for example, is much concerned with the historical development of languages and with linguistic geography.

Charles Fries states, "Most 'linguists' study languages in order to know and to understand their structures—the particular ways in which these languages use their linguistic units to achieve their communicative function. They seek, primarily, knowledge about the units and the working processes of each language, rather than the ability to speak them."[1] Most linguists are fundamentally concerned with studying the spoken language and view it as the quintessential and most revealing form of language; writing is a relatively new invention when compared to the length of time that language has been used in some systematic way for the purpose of communication. Although most current linguists are concerned with language in all aspects of its use, the sounds of language—both as perceived by listeners and, more importantly, as physiologically produced by speakers—are of extraordinary concern to them.

Frank Smith points to some of the limits which surround the field of linguistics: "Linguists in general are concerned with the abstract study of language—they analyze and compare such aspects of languages as their sounds, syntax, and lexicon; they examine similarities and differences among languages, and try to trace their evolutionary development. Linguists are concerned with the nature of language as a system that is available to its users, rather than with the way in which language is acquired, produced, and comprehended by individuals."[2]

Modern linguistics has gathered and organized its information about language according to scientific principles. Modern grammarians (linguists) are concerned with how language operates. They generally do not acknowledge correctness or incorrectness in language; language either communicates or does not communicate. In studying groups that use a given language or dialect, most linguists have concluded that, regardless of the social status of the language or dialect in question, it is sufficient to meet the communicative needs of its users. Within its own context it is effective and appropriate.

Linguistic Terminology

As linguistic influences have been felt in the teaching of reading, reading teachers have had to equip themselves with some of the terminology of linguists in order to understand what linguistically oriented systems were conveying. The following minimal vocabulary of twenty terms will be useful to teachers:

allophone A variant or subclass of a phoneme. For example, the *p* in *put* and in *spire* are allophones; the former is aspirated, the latter unaspirated.

alphabet A set of written symbols which represent the sounds of a language.

alphabetic writing Writing in which graphemes are used to represent the sounds of a language; a highly abstract form of writing.

code The representation of the written language.

decode To identify written letters or words by making graphemic-phonemic correspondences.

dialect A variant form of a root language, usually spoken by members of a given group, social class, or geographic designation, such as the language of the aristocracy, Boston English, British English, ghettoese, Pidgin English.

digraph A pair or group of letters representing a single speech sound, as in m*ea*t, s*ee*m, gra*ph*, *pn*eumonia, and *kn*i*gh*t.

diphthong A blend of a vowel sound with a near-vowel sound as in words like *ai*l, *ou*r, pl*oy, ou*nce; sometimes a diphthong is represented by a single letter, as in *a*le, *u*se, or *i*sle.

graphemes The written representations of sounds; each letter of the alphabet is a grapheme; pictographs and ideographs may also be designated graphemes.

graphemic-phonemic correspondence The relationship which exists between graphemes and their corresponding sounds.

ideographic writing Writing in which a visual symbol represents an idea although nothing about its shape or form as such suggests that idea; the concept *house* may be represented by a symbol which does not look like a house and the concept *man* may be represented by a symbol which does not look like a man.

method of contrast A means of identifying specific phonemes by the comparison and contrast of minimal pairs.

minimal pairs Pairs of words that sound the same except for one phoneme: *day* and *ray, tower* and *power, fall* and *ball.*

morpheme A linguistic unit which carries meaning and contains no smaller meaningful parts, such as *sun, day, pry,* or *port* (free forms) or *port*s, *re*port, sunn*ed,* pry*ing,* dai*ly* (bound forms, since they are dependent upon other forms for their meanings).

phoneme The smallest unit of speech in any language which distinguieshes one utterance from another; *p* distinguishes *pan* from *fan* or from *ban*; *w* distinguishes *west* from *rest* or from *best.*

phonemics The study of sounds (phonemes) in a language that are significant in that they differentiate from each other words which are the same except for one sound: *pet* and *met, pet* and *pen, hoot* and *loot, loot* and *loom.*

phonetics The study of speech sounds as elements of language both as they are conceived physiologically and perceived auditorially.

phonics The study of sound, particularly of graphemic/phonemic relationships which are stressed in some methods of initial reading instruction; may in its early stages stress the sounding of individual letters out of context. Some phonic systems begin with the whole word rather than with its constituent parts.

pictographic writing The oldest form of writing, in which a graphic form looks like the concept it is intended to represent; the pictograph for *house* would resemble a house and that for *man* would resemble a man.

syntax The way in which morphemes are put together into comprehensible patterns.

Linguistic Influences on Reading Instruction

Linguistic science did not exert significant influence upon reading instruction in any organized way until the 1960s, although Leonard Bloomfield's work in the field began as early as 1937[3] and Charles Fries's initial interest in the linguistic implications of reading instruction predated 1960, despite the fact that his *Linguistics and Reading* was not completed until 1962.

By 1960, structural linguistics, a subfield of descriptive linguistics, had received considerable attention by language teachers at all levels; Noam Chomsky had published his historic *Syntactic Structures* three years earlier, and the new transformational/generative grammar which he introduced was beginning to intrigue people interested in language learning. Modern scientific theories about language were proliferating, and concentrated attention was soon to be focused on reading instruction both by the linguists and, yet more intensely, by those who, although not linguists themselves, found the linguists' work with language promising and exciting.

From descriptive linguists like Bloomfield and Fries were to come reassessments of how people learn to decode written language (graphemic representation) and either translate the graphemes into the sounds of language orally or comprehend the graphemes in some meaningful way, that is, get sense out of what they are reading. Dolores Durkin calls decoding "the process of identifying written words on the basis of *grapheme-phoneme correspondences.*"[4] Bloomfield and Fries both developed systems for the initial teaching of reading (decoding), of which more will be said.

During the same period, linguistic geographers and comparative linguists were turning serious attention to the study of dialects. Hans Kurath had made phenomenal progress in cataloguing regional differences in American English in the *Linguistic Atlas of the United States and Canada,* which he edited until his work was taken over by Raven McDavid, Jr., who now serves as senior editor of the *Atlas.* This pioneering work paved the way for sociolinguists, who began to study dialects scientifically and who demonstrated convincingly that all dialects are reasonably regular in their morphology and syntax and that some dialect usages are more regular (*I was, you was, he was,* for example) or more logical (I have three brothers)[5] than comparable constructions in so-called standard English.

The sociolinguists did much to disabuse informed language arts teachers of the notion that one dialect is more correct than another; rather they suggested that one dialect is appropriate for some situations, another appropriate for other situations, just as jeans are fine for a hayride and more formal attire is sensible for a job interview with the vice-president of a bank. Linguists of every bent proclaimed that language is constantly changing (which is why average speakers of English today cannot read *Beowulf* in the original without special instruction) and rejoiced in the fact.

They also pointed out that while some elements of language change, others lag behind; hence we say *nite* but usually write *night,* we say *enuff* but usually write *enough,* we say *dauter* but usually write *daughter.* Each of these words was once pronounced as it is still recorded graphemically. The phonology has now changed, but the graphology has in most cases not reflected the change. Many common words are now obviously in the process of change. *Strength,* with its two bewildering clusters of consonants, is very difficult for most people to pronounce, so while *strength* is still heard, *strenth* and *strent* are not uncommon pronunciations as well. What Charlton Laird wrote in 1953 has been amply supported by the sociolinguists of the 1960s and 1970s: "Speakers of a language take it as they use it, and do not think much about its past or future. They think of it as 'right' or 'wrong,' but they are not much aware that the *wrongs* may become *rights* and the *rights* become *obsoletes.*"[6]

As descriptive linguists and sociolinguists were unraveling some of the puzzles and perplexities of how language operates, psycholinguists were exploring some of the psychological phenomena of how people use language and of what we can glean about the language learning process from the clues provided by normal language use. Among the fruitful investigations motivated by psycholinguistics, perhaps none is quite so important and revealing as miscue analysis.

The remainder of this chapter will deal with the notable contributions of Bloomfield and Fries to reading instruction. Subsequent chapters will deal separately with the influential and expanding areas of miscue analysis and dialectology.

The Bloomfield System

Leonard Bloomfield's own interest in reading instruction was an outgrowth of his experience in helping his own son learn to read. Approaching this problem as a linguistic scientist, he naturally applied the linguistic conventions in which he had been well schooled to the new field in which he sought to achieve a degree of mastery.

Bloomfield begins with the assumption that it is not possible to understand reading without also understanding "the relation of written (or printed) words to speech."[7] He feels that reading can be effectively taught in a much shorter period than is usually required to teach it.

Bloomfield points out the relative newness of reading and writing in comparison to the whole span of human existence and also notes that, even today, more languages exist solely in oral form than exist in written form. He calls writing artificial when compared to speaking. He differentiates among picture writing (pictographic writing), word writing (ideographic writing), and alphabetic writing, noting that the latter is capable of nuances and specificities of which the other two forms of writing are incapable. He notes that once people know the sounds of their language as these sounds are graphemically recorded, they can sound out, with a high degree of uniformity, words of which they do not know the meanings. This is not true of the ideographs which linger in our language—*10* means *ten*; but, whereas readers can sound out *t-e-n,* there is nothing in *10* to tell them how it is pronounced. This is also the case with such signs as *$, ¢, &, 1/2,* and abbreviations such as *Ave., Mr., Apt., Assn., etc.,* etc.

Bloomfield contends with disarming simplicity, "In order to understand the nature of alphabetic writing we need know only what is meant by the term *unit speech sound,* or, as the linguist calls it, by the term *phoneme.*"[8] All human utterances are combinations of phonemes. For those who know the language being spoken, the combinations sound intelligible; for those who do not know the language, the phonemes are meaningless noise. Phonemes in our language, English, have graphemic representations. The twenty-six letters of our alphabet, alone or in combination, yield approximately forty-two sounds of which all English words are composed in one way or another. The sound-letter relationship in English is said to be only about 20 percent efficient,[9] so it is perhaps not surprising that some students have difficulty in learning to read.

Bloomfield removes from the paths of students some of the initial obstacles which the somewhat inefficient sound-letter relationship in English imposes. He begins students with regular words, enabling them to develop strategies for figuring out language before exposing them to irregular words like *was, one, knee, gnu,* or *Phil.* Bloomfield demands that students work systematically with words, beginning with sets or groups of similar two- or three-letter words which differ in only one phoneme: *at, bat, cat, fat, gat, hat, lat, mat, rat*—but never *eat* which totally confuses the issue—or *bud, bug, bum, bun, bus, but,* in which the terminal phoneme distinguishes the words. Bloomfield has no objection to allowing students to pronounce words which are not commonly in the language—*lat* in the list just given—because in doing so they reinforce their ability to make grapheme-phoneme correspondences and also because they will later encounter some of the nonsense syllables in other contexts, such as *lattice.*

Initially Bloomfield would introduce students to all the vowels but to only one pronunciation of each vowel: *a* as in *cat; e* as in *pet; i* as in *pin; o* as in *hot;* and *u* as in *cut.* He would introduce all the consonants except *q* and *x,* but again would introduce them in words in which they have the same sound—if *get* then not *gem*; if *cut,* then not *cent.*

He notes that the list of consonants contains one duplication—*c* as in *cat* and *k*—which are the same phoneme, contending that this will not cause a reading difficulty, although it may cause a spelling difficulty when the student writes. Essentially, the first thing that Bloomfield is aiming for is consistency. The English language is inconsistent, but Bloomfield would isolate consistent elements within it and use these elements in the early stages of reading instruction, allowing students initially to establish a secure and dependable reading base.

Before children are introduced to groups of words, Bloomfield would give them visual discrimination tests and would also ask them to read the letters of the alphabet, first in capital block letters, then in both upper- and lower-case block letters, sounding out each letter.

Part One, then, deals exclusively with groups of two- or three-letter words, all quite regular and consistent in their pronunciation. Part Two, while maintaining the regular pronunciations of each letter, presents words with two (and sometimes three) consecutive consonants which, by sounding the letters as they have learned they sound, students should be able to pronounce: *spit, split, clip, grip, strip,* etc. Later in Part Two, "regular" values are assigned to some more problematic areas of pronunciation: *ing* as in *sing; -nk* as in link; *-sh* and *sh-* as in *fish* or *shot; -ch* or *ch-* as in *inch* or *chin; -th* or *th-* as in *fifth* or *thin; wh-* as in *when; -ck* as in *back;* and *tch* as in *catch.* It should be noted that at the conclusion of Part Two, *is, was, mother, father, brother, than, they,* and *them* have not been introduced because these words contain irregular pronunciations. As has been noted earlier, this limits the content of the reading material, and many teachers have objected that the readings fail to capitalize on the interests of beginning reading students because of the scrupulous omission of irregular sounds. The sentences which Bloomfield and Barnhart have constructed from the words available are no less interesting, however, than those found in more conventional basal-type readers of the period in which these two linguists were writing. Part Two concludes with the introduction of *-x* as in *box* and *qu-* as in *quit.* The spelling of each is treated as regular.

Part Three introduces pairs of vowels (*ee, ea, oo,* etc.) and pairs consisting of a vowel and a semivowel (*ay, aw, ew,* etc.). It is not until Part Four that irregular formations are introduced, and by this time children have developed a good sense of sound-letter correspondence and should be reading the materials in the first three lessons with relative ease and accuracy. As the program grows increasingly more difficult, students have been drilled in large quantities of materials and should have been minimally confused by them because of the consistency of sound-letter correspondences within them.

Teachers have had reservations about the Bloomfield materials because they are not accompanied by illustrations; Bloomfield preferred, for the most part, not to give students a pictographic crutch to lean on while they were attempting to learn alphabetic versions of words. He was explicit in saying that initially students should respond orally to graphemes, lambasting the non-oral method: "The extreme type of ideational method is the so-called 'non-oral' method, where children are not required to pronounce words, but to respond directly to the content. They are shown a printed sentence such as *Skip around the room,* and the correct answer is not to say anything, but to perform the indicated act. Nothing could be less in accord with the nature of our system of writing or with the reading process such as, in the end, it must be acquired."[10] He goes on to excoriate educators who teach by what he calls guesswork rather than according to such scientific principles as those upon which he has based his method.

In retrospect, Bloomfield's contribution to reading instruction added little to the phonics approach which was already in widespread use at the time of his writing. Although he overcame some of the inconsistencies and irregularities of this approach, much undeserved criticism has been laid at his doorstep. For example, Ronald Wardhaugh writes, "Bloomfield emphasizes the relative unimportance of the content of what is read and claims that the child is faced with what is essentially a decoding task. The child already 'knows' the content, for, after all, he can speak the language."[11]

In making this statement, Wardhaugh apparently chose to ignore Fries's explanation: "Bloomfield strove vigorously to avoid mentalistic terms (*concept, idea,* and so forth) in the statement of his linguistic materials and believed that 'Every scientific statement is made in physical terms.' But his efforts to achieve statements in physical rather than 'mentalistic' terms do not lead to the conclusion that he 'ignores meaning' or that 'he takes no account of meaning.'"[12] Fries goes on to reproduce a portion of a letter which Bloomfield sent him in 1945 addressing this very point and making himself quite clear in saying that he regards meaning an essential part of anything having to do with language.

Charles Fries, Linguistics, and Reading

A year after the publication of Bloomfield's and Barnhart's *Let's Read* in 1961, Charles Fries, a linguist of standing comparable to Bloomfield's, completed his notable work *Linguistics and Reading*. As a descriptive, structural linguist, his basic approach was not world-shakingly different from Bloomfield's. Understanding the misinterpretations of Bloomfield's views about comprehension, he was clear to state, "... let us accept *comprehension of the meaning* as our chief objective and attempt to analyze the problems of the sharing of meanings through language."[13] He does warn, however, that "the language is not the meanings or the message; ... A language is the *code of signals* through which various sequences of vocal sounds or speech acts get meaning."[14] He goes on to cite William S. Gray, speaking for the committee which composed the *Second Report of the National Committee on Reading,* in his clear statement that "... reading, as here conceived, includes not only recognition, comprehension, and interpretation, but also the application of the facts apprehended in the study of personal and social problems,"[15] leaving no doubt whatsoever that the reading establishment had taken its stand on the question of comprehension and implying that Fries found this stand neither distasteful nor inconsistent with his own.

Fries contended, "The process of learning to read in one's native language is *the process of transfer* from the auditory signs for language signals which the child has already learned, to the new visual signs for the same signals."[16] His system of teaching was predicated on the idea of transfer and was quite behavioristic: "Learning to read ... means developing a *considerable range of habitual responses* to a specific set of patterns of graphic shapes." He goes on to state a strong pedagogical principle: "The *teaching* of beginning reading to children of four or five must be conceived, not in terms of imparting knowledge, but in terms of opportunities for practice."[17]

Fries gives considerable attention to the sequence of the time and space dimensions in initial reading instruction. The time dimension is largely related to intonation (junctures) in speech, and children must be trained, through Fries's *process of transfer,* to recognize the time dimensions in the printed word. The major space dimension has to do with the fact that English is written horizontally from left to right. This is a basic bit of information which must be recognized by anyone who would read English. Also the direction sequence has to do with the recognition of letters, all but a few of which (H, I, O, and X) must be right side up to have meaning and to be readable in any accurate way.

Fries would use only capital block letters in initial reading instruction, thereby relieving the beginning reader of the somewhat complicated problem of distinguishing letters from each other in both upper and lower case. While he contends that it is necessary for students to be able to distinguish individual letters in the initial stages of reading, Fries does not feel that it is entirely necessary for students to know the names of the letters; recognition is all that counts. He classifies all letters as "stroke letters" (A, E, F, H, I, K, L, M, N, T, V, W, X, Y, and Z), "circle letters" (C, G, O, Q, and S), or "stroke and circle letters" (B, D, J, P, R, and U). He would teach the most commonly used letters initially (omitting Q, Z, X, V, and J) and would teach them contrastively in relation to shape. He calls the initial reading time the "early transfer stage" and introduces as little at this time as students need in order to get along in early reading. From a group of twelve letters, Fries composes thirty-five words typically found in the vocabularies of five-year-olds; he would limit early readings to these words and these letters. Like Bloomfield, he introduces the article *a* at this point, even though it is irregular in its pronunciation. He differs from Bloomfield in that, although *a* is the only vowel he introduces, he presents it in words which require it to be pronounced inconsistently—*FAT, MAN, BAD,* etc. Early on in his system, he emphasizes the contrastive use of minimal pairs.

Fries makes substantial differentiations among the terms, *phonics, phonetics,* and *phonemics,* devoting Chapter Six of *Linguistics and Reading* to this differentiation in such detail that the matter cannot be gone into here in any way that would it justice. While recommending that those interested turn to the chapter itself, it may be helpful here to present Fries's succinct differentiations:

> *Phonics* has been and continues to be a way of teaching beginning reading.
>
> *Phonetics* is a set of techniques by which to identify and describe, in absolute terms, all the differences of sound features that occur in any language.
>
> *Phonemics* is a set of techniques by which to identify and to describe, especially in terms of distribution, the bundles of sound contrasts that constitute the structural units that mark the word-patterns.*18*

Structuralists' Contributions

From people like Bloomfield and Fries came essentially more systematic ways to teach phonics. In 1968, Kenneth Goodman wrote, "What has come to represent the linguistic approach is the kind of updated phonics Bloomfield and Fries devised." Goodman put his finger on one of the major weaknesses of the way in which linguists of the Bloomfield/Fries era approached the teaching of reading, but he places the blame on those in reading who asked linguists ". . . the wrong question: How should reading be taught? They [the linguists] responded with the wrong answer though it was a linguistic one. Linguists should have been asked, 'What do you know about language that will help one understand how reading should be taught?' "*19*

The transformational-generative grammarians, led by Noam Chomsky, whose *Syntactic Structures* (1957) brought about a revolution in the way in which many linguists view language and language learning, have spawned a whole new school of specialists concerned with reading instruction from a linguistic point of view. The psycholinguists, of whom Kenneth Goodman is one, have offered new hope to those who would understand how language operates and how reading instruction is related to the psychological processes involved in language learning. The pioneering work which Goodman and his wife, Yetta, have undertaken in the area of miscue analysis has broad implications for every reading teacher at any level and is the subject of the next chapter.

Chapter 7
MISCUE ANALYSIS[1]

Writing in 1968, Ronald Wardhaugh quite correctly asserted, "There is something very important missing from the work that has been done so far in applying linguistic knowledge to reading instruction, and that missing element is the linguistic knowledge acquired over the past decade. The kind of linguistics which is partially introduced into some versions of the linguisitic method is Bloomfieldian linguistics; however, beginning with the publication of Chomsky's *Syntactic Structures*[1a] in 1957, linguistics has undergone a revolution." Wardhaugh continues, "It would not be fair to say that Bloomfieldian linguistics is dead or even moribund; but, to use the current idiom, it is not where the action is."[2]

Wardhaugh goes on to applaud the new linguists, the transformational-generative grammarians because of their interest in making "a distinction between the skills and competency a person must have to behave linguistically and his actual observed linguistic behavior."[3] Wardhaugh then ventures to speculate on some of the ways in which the transformational-grammarians might shed light on the teaching of reading and prophetically suggests, among other things, "Even mistakes should be thought of as applications of wrong rules, as evidence of faulty processing, rather than as instances of random behavior."[4] Wardhaugh cannot be credited, because of this statement, with fathering the miscue analysis movement, since Kenneth and Yetta Goodman were already beginning their investigations in this area and were applying some of the fruits of the transformational-generative grammarians to their researches. Kenneth Goodman had also already published *The Psycholinguistic Nature of the Reading Process,*[4a] and Wardhaugh was certainly familiar with this seminal book.

In the two decades since the publication of *Syntactic Structures,* Chomsky's impact has been felt in many areas of learning and investigation. Chomsky's exploration into the question of how all the syntactic structures of any language are generated from basic kernel sentences focused attention upon the underlying psychology of syntactic generation and inaugurated the intensive study of psycholingistics.

As the psycholinguists turned their attention to areas of human communication previously unexplored from a psycholinguistic standpoint, a new and broader understanding of language skills was developed. Many of the emerging researchers in this area came early to realize that the acquisition of language skills, notably of reading and writing, follows psycholinguistic patterns which fit into certain broad categories. Subsequent research has provided many challenging insights into the patterns of language learning; however, some of the most important research has, because of its specialized nature and difficulty of interpretation and understanding, failed to reach classroom teachers who could profit significantly from many of its findings.

What Is Miscue Analysis?

This chapter will focus on *miscue analysis,* a term coined by Kenneth Goodman as an outgrowth of his investigation into the sorts of errors students make in oral reading and of what these errors tell about the reading characteristics of the people who make them. A miscue, as Goodman uses the term, is merely an error or inaccuracy in either oral or silent reading. Goodman elects to use the term "miscue" because "miscues are not simply errors, but the results of the reading process having miscarried in some minor or major ways." Goodman continues, "The phenomena to be dealt with will be called miscues, rather than errors, in order to avoid the negative connotation of errors (all miscues are not bad) and to avoid the implication that good reading does not include miscues."[5]

Teachers can learn a great deal from the miscues that occur in the reading their students do. They can assess miscues only in oral reading, but such miscues can also suggest the types of problems their students may be having in silent reading. It is important that teachers heed Goodman's admonition "that only in rare special circumstances is oral reading free of miscues and that silent reading is never miscue-free."[6] More importantly, the teacher must hearken well to Goodman's research-based caveat that "it appears likely that a reader who requires perfection in his reading will be a rather inefficient reader."[7]

Three Types of Information the Reader Must Process

According to Goodman, when readers react to graphic displays (writing) on a page, they must process three types of information: grapho-phonic, syntactic, and semantic. Sometimes they must process all three types of information simultaneously, sometimes not. Syntactic information is processed in regard to syntactic structures such as phrases, clauses, etc. For example, a reader who reads "nip" for "pin" or, more commonly in oral reading and speaking, the metathesized "irrelevancy" for "irrelevancy" is processing grapho-phonic and, possibly, semantic information, whereas the reader who renders "They have done a good day's work" as "They had did a good day's work" is processing syntactic information and likely is miscuing because of dialect interference.

Students who are reading silently are decoding, translating graphic markings on a page into meaningful units. Probably the most efficient readers—that is, those in the top one or two percent nationally in reading ability and reading efficiency—are engaged largely in a decoding process. Yet even these readers, in their silent reading, engage in some subvocalization. Any vocalization, whether reading aloud or subvocalizing in silent reading, involves a more complicated process than decoding; it requires decoding of the graphic representation and then encoding of the sound for which the graphic representation stands. This process slows readers down, although in some cases it may not work to the detriment of their efficiency. Readers encountering for the first time new words (*miniseries, subarea, kinesics,* for example) or complicated words (*Zoroastrianism, shenanigan, neuropsychiatric,* for example) usually have to vocalize them in order to be able to deal with them. If they cannot deal with them within a context, then their reading efficiency (comprehension) is reduced.

On the other hand, some readers need to vocalize every word in silent reading, and in so doing they slow their reading pace to the point that they cannot derive the meaning from a paragraph or, perhaps, even from a sentence or a phrase. It is important for the teacher of reading to recognize the kinds of processes that are going on in reading and, having identified them, to know how to use them diagnostically to determine what individual students require.

Two Basic Categories of Miscuing

Although Goodman has identified twenty-eight different categories of miscues,[8] let us consider at this point two major areas in which miscues are detected and consider further how teachers can use the information that these miscues provide to determine the type and gravity of the reading problems that students have.

Frank Smith[9] (as well as Goodman,[10] Burke and Goodman,[11] and Weber[12]) has noted that proficient beginning readers make as many miscues as beginning readers who are not proficient, but that their miscues are of a different nature from those made by their less proficient classmates. He reports, "The errors of less proficient readers typically reflect a good deal of the graphic information in the written text (for example, 'saw' for 'was', 'butter' for 'batter') but they make little sense in the context of the passage as a whole. More accomplished readers tend to make errors that may appear quite gross visually—omitting, substituting, or rearranging entire sequences of words—but that nonetheless retain the underlying meaning of the passage read. They do not stop to sound out or even identify individual words."[13]

Obviously, the student who reads, "She went to a moving in wont" for "She went to a movie in town," and goes right on reading, has a much greater and more disabling reading problem than the student who reads, "There is some*one* in the house" for "There is some*body* in the house" or "They live happily in the forest" for "They live in the forest happily." The latter reader is also distinguishable from the former because he/she, in making a miscue like "She crust the day she was born," will go back and reread, "She curst the day she was born," realizing that the first rendering of the sentence does not make sense.

In determining the extent and type of students' reading problems, teachers must pay careful attention to what happens when students are reading orally. They must also bear in mind Goodman's earlier noted comment that readers who demand perfection of themselves are likely inefficient readers.

Reading as Information Processing

In one of his early articles, Goodman asserts, "A proficient reader is one so efficient in sampling and predicting that he uses the least (not the most) available information necessary."[14] In other words, really proficient readers can comprehend accurately what they are reading without laboring over it. The eye feeds the graphic representation to the mind which instantly, and probably nonverbally in many cases, processes it. The flow to the mind is constant and rapid; the units communicated are relatively large units, "secondary school" rather than "se-con-da-ry sc-ho-ol" or "s-e-c-o-n-d-a-r-y s-c-h-o-o-l." Very likely proficient readers are engaging the right hemisphere of the brain in the reading process as well as the left, allowing the *gestalt* of words and phrases to aid in their processing for greater efficiency and accuracy.

Goodman describes reading as "a psycholinguistic process, in which meaning is decoded from a linguistic medium of communication."[15] The linguistic medium of communication alluded to here is presumably graphic representation or writing unless one wishes to go so far as to say that deriving meaning from a painting, let us say, is a form of reading. The definition would be a very common-place one, in essence, "Reading is decoding writing," were it not for the inclusion of the words "psycholinguistic process." These words move the definition into a new arena, one very much concerned with the question of how the mind works on language and with the converse question of how language works on the mind. It is this qualification in Goodman's definition that makes the definition unique and should help teachers to be more aware of the learning problems some of their students have. The student who sees in the mind's eye "secondary school" or "secondaryschool" can process that particular piece of information fifteen times faster than the student who sees "s-e-c-o-n-d-a-r-y s-c-h-o-o-l." And, perhaps more importantly, the former student has the mental concept of "secondary school" in mind when he/she pushes on to the next word or phrase. The latter student moves on to the next word or phrase in the same laborious way that he/she attacked "s-e-c-o-n-d-a-r-y s-c-h-o-o-l" and cannot derive meaning from the material being read. Such a student is, in effect, and for all practical purposes, a nonreader.

Teachers beyond the primary grades who encounter such students are faced with enormous problems, some of them stemming from early training that stressed a narrow phonics emphasis over the reading of whole words. For some students the early damage may be all but irreversible. For others, new approaches to reading—and these new approaches must involve a great deal of eye training—may yield results. A first step would be to surround such students with large signs, clearly printed, identifying objects around the classroom—desk, door, chair, window, clock, etc.—and to engage them in games involving words. For example, on large cards, clearly printed commands such as "Look Left" or "Stand Up" or "Touch Your Nose" might be written. The teacher flashes a card. The first student to obey the command gets to flash the next card. Such activities will encourage some students to see and process larger entities than they have been able to process previously. If students cannot handle commands, try writing just one word on each card and begin by saying, "Touch whatever part of you is written on the card"; then flash *ear, nose, chin, eye, toe,* and graduate to *wrist, ankle, finger, stomach,* and other more difficult words. The teacher might start another exercise by saying, "Point to whatever is written on the card," and continue with words such as *door, wall, floor, boy, desk,* then proceed to more difficult words like *light, ceiling, eraser, cupboard, chalkboard,* etc.

It should be remembered that post-primary school students who have severe reading deficits are, for the most part, ashamed of those deficits. Their shame may manifest itself in various ways—apathy, defensiveness, lack of cooperation. Such students have, characteristically, learned not to take risks within the academic setting because their risks have not paid off in the past. If anything is to succeed in helping them to cope with and overcome their problems, it must be presented to them in a nonthreatening and nonjudgmental context. In the excitement of a game, students lose their self-consciousness and perform more effectively than they would in a more typical classroom setting.

Reading Miscues and Dialects

Teachers working with students brought up in environments where dialects predominate which vary significantly from so-called standard English must have some understanding of their students' dialects if they are to judge whether students are actually miscuing in oral reading or whether they are merely making substitutions from their own dialects. In most rural areas of Piedmont, North Carolina, for example, a student who reads "Maybe I can go if the rain stops" as "I might can go if the rain stops" is translating the more standard expression into the dialect of the region. W. Nelson Francis has noted that students whose dialects differ greatly from that in the works they are trying to read may have considerable trouble in learning to read.[16] However, the child whose teacher knows some of the dialects of the community will stand a better chance of learning to read than the child whose teacher is in ignorance of these dialects.

Kenneth R. Johnson has made useful generalizations on sounds that black children use in certain words, particularly those ending in /th/ as in words like *birth,* which in Black dialect is *birf.* He has also noted other consistent patterns which it is necessary for teachers of reading to recognize.[17] Johnson quite correctly reminds the reader, "Black English is *not* 'sloppy' English spoken by children with 'lazy lips and lazy tongues'; it is a structured, functional variety of English, and it should not be stigmatized."[18] What Johnson says of Black dialect may be said with equal validity about most other dialects of English.

Teachers need to recognize that students may make substitutions into their own dialects. Labov notes, "If a student reads *He always looked for trouble when he read the news* as *He a'way look' fo' trouble when he read* (rhyming with *bed*) *de news,* the teacher should be able to judge that he is reading correctly."[19] Such a rendering is reading correctly *within the confines and pronunciation system of a student's own dialect.* Teachers need also to remember that if the task at hand is to teach reading to students who are having difficulty mastering this skill, *the focus should be on reading.* If the student reads "have did" for "have done," this is not the time for a grammar lesson which would only divert student attention from the task at hand. In trying to teach several things at once, teachers reduce the efficiency with which slower students learn.

One might bear in mind a sequence in Dorothy Heathcote's superb film, *Three Looms Waiting,*[20] in which Ms. Heathcote is helping students to enact a prisoner-of-war scene. She tells the students that as prisoners-of-war they will be grilled by their captors. Then she begins grilling a boy: "What work did you do before the war?" "I was a lorry driver." "Is your father alive?" "No, Ma'am." "How did he die?" "He was killed in the war, ma'am." "Where did he live?" "In London." "Where in London?" "Coventry, ma'am." "And is your mother alive?"

In the critique of this session which followed, Ms. Heathcote was asked, "Why did you not tell the boy that Coventry is not a part of London?" She replied, "Because I don't give a damn where Coventry is. I was not giving a geography lesson. I was trying to help a young boy to know what it feels like to be a prisoner, an alien in a foreign land, and at that moment he was beginning to know what it felt like. I could not interrupt the development of this feeling to tell him where Coventry is." Too many teachers forget that focus can be destroyed if the lesson deviates from its intended objective(s) in order to provide information which the student does not at that particular moment need.

Teachers of reading need to remember Goodman's words: "(1) Phonemes do not really exist outside of the full system of restraints in which they are found [and] (2) oral language is no less a code than written language."[21] Indeed, when oral response is produced from graphic representation (reading from printed material), the reader is involved in a process that is very complex psychologically and is called upon to juggle two or more coding challenges simultaneously. While the process is an easy and natural one for proficient readers (which most teachers are and have been since their earliest recollections), it can be an incredibly difficult, intimidating, and discouraging process to the deficient reader. If teachers do not understand this fully (and it is difficult to understand why others have trouble doing the things that one does easily and well), they are not in a position to teach reading to people with reading handicaps.

Dealing with Miscues in Oral Reading

As we have seen, miscues are a natural part of all reading, oral or silent. If the aim in oral reading is perfection, then every miscue or error must be corrected. However, to do this will be discouraging to students and will do little to help them to be better readers. Rather, it will destroy in them any desire to read. Teachers need to be quick to recognize the types of miscues that students make and to know that some require attention while others do not. Tortelli writes, "Since most readers are speakers of the language they read, they bring to the process of reading an intuitive knowledge of oral language that facilitates their getting meaning from written language."*22*

Probably the best criterion that teachers can apply in reaching decisions about whether to correct students' miscues is that of meaning—does the reader understand what he/she is reading? The oral language which students are accustomed to hearing may differ quite substantially from the written language to which they are exposed in reading. Many students, while they are decoding from the printed page, are simultaneously encoding into their own dialects, making the standard English on the page conform systematically to the conventions of those dialects. On a rather simple level, *ten* may come out *tin*, not because the reader cannot differentiate between the two words of this minimal pair but because he/she does not make an audible distinction in his/her normal pronunciation of the two words. In such situations, even though both words may be pronounced identically, context will reveal which is intended. On a more sophisticated level, standard English "it does" or "she doesn't" may come out "it do" or "she don't" (or even, "she don' ") because the reader will translate the standard expression into the corresponding dialect locution. Such a deviation from the printed text is not an error to be corrected *if the purpose of oral reading is to determine whether the reader is able to read a text with meaning.* Teaching the differences that exist among dialects may be appropriate ultimately in a student's linguistic development, but teachers need to learn not to confuse students by drifting into teaching a second major lesson because something being done in the primary major lesson suggests it.

Laray Brown writes of a black child who made no differentiation between *him* and *hem* in oral reading, pronouncing both words /him/. Brown asks, "Did he mispronounce all words with these two vowels in similar environments—for example, *pin* and *pen*?" Brown continues, "The answer was yes. Consequently, I said that I would not have corrected the Black child and that I would have corrected the White child [making the same miscue]. I feel that one must consider with which language system one is working. the Black English (BE) or the Standard English (SE) system."*23* While many traditionalists rebel against this

62

point of view, it is linguistically and pedagogically a sound one. The question is not whether so-called standard usage (Network Standard) *should* be taught; eventually students obviously will profit from being introduced to it. However, in the initial stages of reading instruction, the focus should be on decoding and comprehending, not upon the subtleties of dialect differences.

Brown correctly contends that speakers of dialects such as Black English have a passive knowledge and understanding of standard English sufficient for them to be able to comprehend it. He cites tests "where children were asked to repeat sentences that they were given orally [in which] Black children 'digested' the given SE forms and rendered translations in BE with the same meaning." Therefore, Brown contends, ". . . failure of some Black children to learn to read is not due primarily to dialectal differences. I see no reason that a child need to have more than a passive knowledge of SE to learn to read."[24]

Emotions concerning this issue have run so high that the results of reliable and meticulous linguistic studies have been obscured by the emotional involvement of teachers and parents who feel that every language problem must be worked on simultaneously despite the existence of convincing research evidence that learning will be diminished when this is done.

Aaron Lipton, writing two years before Brown, substantiates the fact that "as children call out substituted words, they *may* actually *see* and *know* the words as they are written, but find it more linguistically comfortable to say the words as they do." Lipton warns, "In many instances in forcing a child to call words accurately by continual reference to his errors and correction of them, we deny him the opportunity to read within the framework of his own language development. This condition has caused many children to avoid reading and to become failures with the reading process."[25]

Be it not thought that Brown, Lipton, or this writer believe for a moment that any child should be locked into one dialect for the whole of his or her educational experience. The plea is that children be allowed the right to their own language while they are trying to master the elementary forms of some of the basic skills of that language. When children can function unselfconsciously in the areas of speaking, reading, and writing, then attention can profitably be turned to questions of the different usages and conventions that exist within the broad range of English language dialects.

Gaining Information Through Miscues

Perceptive teachers will learn a great deal about their students' ability to cope with language if they know how to interpret the miscues which students make in oral reading. It takes linguistic sophistication to read and simultaneously translate into another dialect, and many primary school students are easily able to do this. Such linguistic flexibility should be valued rather than condemned.

Tortelli recommends that primary teachers make individual diagnoses of their students by having each student read aloud to them an unfamiliar story of which the teacher has a copy. The teacher is to write on his/her copy every word that the student utters which is not in the original text or which differs from the original text. Omissions of words are also to be noted.

The teacher is then to place horizontally on a sheet of paper four column headings labeled "Unexpected Readings" (substitution of words or any other deviations from the text), "Intended Readings," "Language," and "Meaning."

The paper would then be numbered vertically from one to ten, and the first ten unexpected calls would be recorded. If the student read "hurt" for "hit" as the verb in the first sentence, "A big boy hit Nan," then "hurt" would be recorded under column one, "Unexpected Readings." The word "hit" would be recorded under column two, "Intended Readings." Under column three would be recorded a "yes" because the substitution resulted in a grammatically acceptable sentence. In most cases "A big boy hit Nan" could be rendered "A big boy hurt Nan" with little grammatical problem, whereas "Them big boy hit/hurt Nan" might indicate a grammatical inconsistency (depending on the reader's dialect), indicating that the reader had made a miscue which is not meaningful in terms of the sense of the sentence. Under column four, "Meaning," a "no" would be recorded if either the word "Them" or "hurt" had been the substitution, because the original meaning would not have been conveyed in either case.[26]

In order to obtain the most valid information from students who read to teachers individually, Goodman recommends that the reading should be somewhat difficult for the student, a bit above his/her level, and that it should be long enough to generate twenty-five or more miscues. Goodman would have the reading recorded on a tape or cassette for later replay; he would have the student retell the story immediately after having read it to check for comprehension. The miscues would be coded with the use of Taxonomy, Reading Miscue Inventory, or other such means so that they might be viewed analytically and diagnosed in terms of the student's geographical origins, ethnic background, etc.[27]

Teachers should always pay close attention to the level of miscuing. Calling "don't" for "do not" is not a serious miscue. It will not distort meaning even though it may alter the style of what has been written in some minute way. Pronouncing a word in dialect (*idear* for *idea*) is a miscue hardly worth considering with beginning readers. Inability to distinguish consistently between *them* and *they* or between *him* and *his* is a problem of greater magnitude, because it might alter meaning. Omitting words, particularly descriptive words such as reading "A boy hit the girl" rather than "A big boy hit the girl," may, if not checked, cause future problems in comprehension. Misreading "was" as "saw" may, if done consistently, indicate problems connected with mixed dominance, a common cause of serious reading handicaps. Similarly, having difficulty distinguishing between "m" and "w" may suggest a like problem. Reading "brain" for "train" is more serious than reading "goin' " for "going" or "gonna" for "going to."

Teachers in time come to know their students well enough to be able to judge their reading performances in the broad contexts of their lives and environments. No single set of criteria will work for all children, obviously. It is the teacher's job—and a great challenge it is—to be able to assess the individual situations of all students in the classroom and to work with all these students to help them overcome the specific stumbling blocks which stand between them and the highest level of achievement of which each is capable.

Using Miscue Information

Armed with an understanding of how to categorize miscues in oral reading, teachers can begin to classify the types of reading problems that many of their students have. They can also make certain broad decisions about which students have legitimately handicapping reading problems and which students, even though they make miscues, derive the basic meaning from most of what they read and read it with sufficient speed and efficiency that they are adequate readers.

Yetta Goodman, addressing teachers at the elementary school level, says, "There is no question that certain types of miscues are of higher order than others; miscues of low order give way to miscues of higher order as children become more proficient readers. Miscues must not be looked upon as mistakes which are bad and should be eradicated but as overt behaviors which may unlock aspects of intellectual processing. . . . Miscues in reading give insight into the reading process."[27] But if miscues are to provide teachers with insights into the reading process, then teachers must have a sophisticated knowledge of how and why the student is miscuing. They must know when correction is appropriate and when it is not. They must also seek to provide their students with ideas and concepts that are at their maturity level as the process of teaching reading advances. Frequent discussion activities allow students with reading deficits to function in situations in which they can experience a feeling of success and accomplishment for which they are not dependent upon reading skills, and this very sense of accomplishment may be the spur that will make them put forth the extra effort necessary to expend if they are ever to become efficient readers.

Chapter 8

DIALECTS AND EARLY READING INSTRUCTION

We have learned in the preceding chapter on miscue analysis that probably no efficient sustained reading, oral or silent, is wholly free from miscues. Using the least rather than the most information available to differentiate one word from another leads to efficient reading habits; it also makes miscues inevitable. Written English is in itself a unique dialect quite different in many particulars from any form of spoken English. However, English written in the so-called Standard Dialect bears a closer resemblance, obviously, on the levels of both its graphemic/phonemic and syntactic correspondences, to spoken language of the same dialect than it does, let us say, to southern dialect, New England dialect, or any other dialect of English that one might mention.

Dialects and Status

Linguists have amply demonstrated that all established dialects which have ever been studied by them follow consistent patterns, no matter how much at variance such patterns might be from the patterns found in the version of the mother language which is spoken by those who control the society. They contend that every language, as well as every dialect of language, is sufficient for the communication needs of the group using it. Whatever is spoken by the controlling class comes to be viewed as standard. As power shifts, fashions change. For example, French was the polite language in England from the time of the Norman Conquest until some two or three centuries following; English was held in low regard, as were those who spoke it. The presidential administration of John Kennedy helped to add status to a New England dialect already pretty well accepted because that region of the country had produced many national leaders through the years, right from our nation's beginnings. The aura surrounding the New England dialect is an aura of power. Jimmy Carter's rise to power has caused many people to have a more tolerant attitude than was common a quarter of a century ago toward the southern dialect commonly used in rural Georgia. British English, which is probably as deviant from the Network Standard Dialect of the United States as is Black English, is quite favorably received by most Americans for so complex a variety of psychological and social reasons that to chart them in any exhaustive way would be a virtual impossibility.

It is interesting to note that in London or Leeds or Liverpool, the Scottish dialect stigmatizes its users just as Black dialect can stigmatize its users in some white middle-class situations in the United States. The same Americans who show a negative emotional reaction to Black dialect might find charming the very Scottish dialect which makes a proper Londoner cringe. There is little logic to such reactions, although there usually exists an intricate history to account for them, and this history often reaches far back into ill-remembered time. We all carry with us language prejudices, both pro and con, which we cannot begin to understand—or even, in some cases, to recognize.

Black Dialect

Black English is a legitimate and systematic form of the English language. Valid grammatical generalizations can be made about its structure, conventions, and use. Among these generalizations are the following:

1. Omission of *'s* in possessives: *That is my sister book. Where Mary car at?*

2. Regularization of third person singular: *That dude run real fast. Do he have my check?*

3. Regularization of strong verbs: *throwed* for *threw, have did* for *have done.*

4. Dropping of *-s* after a plural marker: *Hey, Sally, can I have ten cent? Those (Dose) three dude be crazy.* [In the second example, notice the double plural markers, *Those* and *three*. Also note that Standard Dialect omits the plural *-s* in some situations: *I want a ten-cent candy bar. Do you have a fifty-cent piece?* but not in others: *Give me fifty cents.*]

5. Omission of terminal *-ed* in the past tense: *Mercy me, I cook all day last Sunday. I change that tire yesterday.* [Again note the avoidance of redundancy.]

6. Not rendering the past conditional question: *Alice ask can I come to the party* not *Alice asked if I might come to the party.*

7. Use of the *be* copula rather than *is: I be here every day till six.* The copula may also be omitted (deleted zero form), but this is done only where Standard English would use a contraction. Black English may use the contraction, but it more often omits the copula: *He's going home* may be rendered as it stands, but more usually in Black English will be rendered *He goin' home.* The deletion never occurs in instances where Standard English cannot accommodate a contraction: *I don't know where he is* cannot, in Standard English, be *I don't know where he's;* hence in Black English it would be rendered *I don't know where he at* or *I don't know where he be.*[1]

8. Omission of the copula as in the second example in number 1: *Where Mary car at?* OR *There (Dere) my house. Man, you in my seat.*

9. Dropping of prefixes: *'til for until; 'zausted* for *exhausted; 'spired* for *inspired.*

10. Omission of final consonants *k, p,* and *t* preceded by *s: desk, pest, lisp* becomes *des', pes',* and *lis'.*

11. Substitution of /f/ for /th/ in words like *with (wif)* and *teeth (teef).*

12. Substitution of initial /th/ with /d/ or /t/: *dere* for *there; dose* for *those; trew* for *through.*[2]

13. Subject reiteration: *John, he come to see me. My mamma, she a big lady. Mary car, it won' go.*

The foregoing usages are standard within the dialect context in which they occur. This does not make them acceptable in or appropriate to all situations; however, linguistically speaking, they are neither correct nor incorrect. They fulfill the criterion of intelligibility to other speakers of the same dialect. They permit communication. Any judgments about their correctness would necessarily be social rather than linguistic. While social judgments cannot be ignored, neither can they be permitted to cloud the situation in planning early language learning experiences such as initial reading instruction.

Common Sense Would Tell You

Common sense would indicate that in the early stages of reading instruction, children whose dialect is dramatically different from that of the materials they are expected to read might be taught much more effectively if early reading materials were in their own dialect, rather than in Standard English. As we have noted earlier in this chapter, written English is in itself a dialectal variant of spoken English. It would seem only sensible that children who have to deal not only with the inherent dialectal variations between written and spoken English but also with that between Standard English and the English which they are most used to hearing and which they themselves speak enter their initial reading situations at a double disadvantage.

Linguists like Joan Baratz, Roger Shuy, and William Stewart reflected on this problem, as did many of their colleagues, and made a persuasive case for the use of dialect readers; that is, for beginning readers which present the same story in both Black dialect and Standard English. Judy Schwartz reports, "The first practical application of this approach occurred earlier, in 1968, when the Board of Education of the City of Chicago published a series of experimental readers in which half of the content was written in black dialect."[3] A year later, Steptoe published *Stevie*,[4] in which the basic text is in Standard English but the dialogue is all in Black dialect. By the next year, the Education Study Center had published three dialect readers[5] in which stories were presented in Black dialect and, in control volumes identical in everything but the text, in Standard English. *Ollie* reads, "Here go Ollie./Ollie have a big family./He have three sisters./A sister name Brenda." The control volume reads, "This is Ollie./Ollie has a big family./He has three sisters./A sister named Brenda, etc."

Common sense once had people convinced that the earth was flat, that the universe was geocentric, and that people could never leave the environment of their own planet, Earth. We have lived to see all these common sense hypotheses shattered. It now appears evident that the common sense idea of using Black dialect readers with students who speak Black dialect as a means of helping them to be better readers is about to be exploded, even though the linguistic hypotheses on which the theory rested were appealing and understandable ones.

But before we get into a discussion of the research which has tested these hypotheses, let us consider public reactions to the introduction of dialect readers.

Public Reactions to Dialect Readers

Emotions have run very high in situations where Black dialect readers have been used in initial reading instruction. Most extremely negative reactions against dialect readers came from people with little or no formal exposure to linguistic theory, so that their objections were based upon other than linguistic considerations. Judy Schwartz has done a provocative attitudinal survey focusing on the reception of Black dialect materials by a sampling of sixty-nine people categorized by occupation, race, and socioeconomic status (SES). She hypothesized that those expressing favorable attitudes would be teachers and other education-related professionals, as well as white respondents of average socioeconomic status. She hypothesized that those expressing unfavorable opinions would be paraprofessionals, Blacks, and those of low socioeconomic status.[6]

Although the Schwartz study found that "the use of black dialect materials for beginning reading instruction, especially as a transitional medium and when used in conjunction with standard dialect materials, is perceived postively by both black and white people,"[7] the researchers elicited some very negative responses from the respondents: ". . . good English is good English, and bad English is bad English, no matter who is speaking it. There is no such thing as black language." Schwartz says, "Most respondents, regardless of category of occupation, race, and SES, demonstrated an incomplete or inaccurate understanding of black dialect. Among the terms used to describe it were: broken English, the wrong way, incorrect, not proper, slang, bad English, play talk. One black paraprofessional characterized black English as '. . . a short easy way out.' "[8] Certainly the responses indicate that people have little knowledge of the linguistic status of Black English—and probably of most other dialects of English. They are judgmental in ways that no linguist could be.

Perhaps those most troubled by Black dialect materials were Black parents, many of whom felt that the future hope for their children rested in their being educated in the same way as mainstream American society so that they would ultimately have upward social mobility within the context of mainstream America. Speaking of dialect materials, Schwartz says, "Almost as quickly as they appeared . . . they vanished from the scene usually in the midst of a heated debate in which the move to use such readers was characterized as an attempt at racial stereotyping. Typically, the strongest opponents were middle-class blacks."[9]

Dorothy Strickland voiced strenuous objections to the use of dialect materials for a number of reasons, one of which was that "Most black parents object to the use of such books as initial instructional materials for reading." She worried that the continued use of such materials threatened "the potential erosion of school/community relations and the resultant disruption in the learning process which would follow."[10] William Stewart answers this objection somewhat less than convincingly: "It is difficult for me to see . . . especially given the attitudinal and cultural autonomy of lower-class black children vis-à-vis their parents, how parental hostility to any particular teaching strategy could offset whatever in-school pedagogical advantages the teaching strategy might have."[11] This statement apparently overlooks the structure of the Black family. It suggests to this writer that Stewart would give the schools totalitarian powers to teach students as and what they like if, in the school's eyes, learning would proceed therefrom. The voices of parents, it seems he is suggesting, should not be heeded.

Strickland also expresses an understandable concern about Black dialect readers because there is not a single Black dialect "which all black disadvantaged children speak."[12] Strickland is not opposed to using dialect materials in classrooms, but she suggests moderately, and it seems wisely, that initial reading materials be "based on the individual child's own language. . . . Personal experience stories using the child's dictation as the content and the teacher as scribe can serve as an important tool for introducing reading."*13*

This exercise might be taken one step further. Teachers or other students might translate such stories "the way Johnny or Mary or Sandra or Mark would tell them." In classes that are racially and culturally diverse, this sort of exercise is enormously valuable because it involves students in working with point of view, with language and syntactic variety, and with authentic revising, one of the highest and most productive forms of which is that of preparing a story for a different audience than that for which it was originally written.

Do Dialect Readers Really Help?

Research on the effectiveness of dialect readers is still insufficient to permit any valid generalizations to be made about their overall usefulness in helping dialect speakers to learn how to read well. As was noted in the preceding chapter, a passive understanding of Standard English appears to be all that dialect speakers need in order to learn how to read. While acknowledging the difference between Standard English and Black English, Jane Torrey concludes, ". . . the difference in phonology between standard English and black English is not directly relevant to reading. *All* children who learn to read English have to break a fairly complex code of sound-spelling relationships. The fact that the correspondences are different for speakers of Afro-American does not in itself prove that they are more difficult than for standard speakers."*14* Torrey's thesis is "that the functional aspects of language have more serious implications for illiteracy than the structural ones." She goes on to say unabashedly, "A passive understanding of standard dialect should suffice for purposes of learning to read, *even if a given child never learns to use the standard forms of speech.*"*15*

It should be remembered, for example, that most southern students entering school are exposed to reading materials in a dialect other than their natural one, yet their passive understanding of the version of English found in their initial reading materials is sufficient to enable them to read the materials at hand. The writer is aware of no serious suggestions that initial reading materials be prepared in southern, midwestern, or New England dialect, and the absence of such suggestions stems from the fact that it has long been recognized that students speaking such dialects can make the transfer to the language of their initial readers because their passive understanding of Standard English is sufficient to permit this transfer.

Herbert D. Simons and Kenneth R. Johnson (the latter a native speaker of Black English) have recently completed and reported on a research study of sixty-seven second and third grade Black children in Oakland, California, all of whom were users of some form of the Black English dialect. The study is an intriguing one, going as it does into many aspects of dialect interference in early reading experiences. This carefully constructed study, while it cannot be viewed as conclusive for a number of reasons which the experimenters clearly identify, "provides no evidence that second and third grade dialect-speaking Black children read dialect texts any better than they read standard texts."*16* This single conclusion, the most important one reached in the study, flies in the face of what many prominent linguists have believed and runs quite counter to what this writer would have expected such research to reveal. It is clear that the need exists for considerable research of this kind which will involve a much larger and much more diverse sampling. The Simons/Johnson materials provide a significant initial step, and their findings are important.

What Language Abilities Do Dialect Speakers Possess?

Considerable speculation has been engaged in regarding whether disadvantaged dialect speakers begin school with a sufficient command of oral language to make initial reading instruction feasible for them. Martin Deutsch contended in 1963 that failure in reading among disadvantaged children is attributable to their having had insufficient experiences with vocabulary and syntax.[17] Some years later, Engelmann contended that the average child from a low socioeconomic background has no linguistic concepts and cannot understand the meaning of common words.[18] More recently, Christopher Clausen has written, apparently completely in ignorance of all that recent research has revealed about language, "By any reasonable measure, Standard English is intellectually superior to any dialect in that it gives its users the resources for a broader range of communication, whether informational or emotional. The standard language has a larger vocabulary and more varied structures than any dialect."[19] Apparently it does not bother Clausen that what he has written is patently and demonstrably untrue.

One might argue conversely that, because they have a passive understanding of Standard English and an active understanding of their own dialects, dialect speakers, particularly Black dialect speakers, have a broader vocabulary range and a greater variety of syntactic structures available to them, passively at least, than speakers of so-called Network Standard. One might also quarrel with Clausen whose argument, if logically extended, would necessarily conclude, for example, that standard Arabic is inferior to Standard English because it lacks some of the constructions, such as the past conditional, which all dialects of English contain. Such an argument could also lead to the conclusion that modern Russian, Polish, or Lithuanian are superior to Standard English because these languages have a more intricate nominal case structure and a more highly developed system of verbal aspects than English can boast. Obviously, such an argument would not be linguistically acceptable any more than Clausen's argument is. Judgments such as these are in no way valid and grow out of prejudice, gut feelings, and a total misunderstanding of available linguistic data. They obscure rather than enlighten. They are elitist in nature and reveal a surprising lack of historical perspective in the view of language which they present.

An unfortunate aspect of so much that has been written about the differences between Standard English and Black English is that it has been written from the standpoint of Standard English as the model and as superior, which makes any argument that might follow specious if not downright invalid. It seems to matter little whether the writers are white or black; many of them make value judgments which have no place in any serious inquiry into the matter of how speakers of a dialect can best be taught the language skills, including reading, which will enable them to function adequately in their society.

Beatrice K. Levy, in a splendid study, reports on a research project which she conducted with a group of twenty first grade students from the Brownsville section of New York City. All the subjects were black, all were from families of low socioeconomic status. Levy sought to test these children in three areas affecting language: "(1) vocabulary, (2) the mean length of T-units, and (3) three structures within T-units."[20]

Levy compared her findings with those of Roy O'Donnell, William Griffin, and Raymond Norris who made a similar survey of white, middle-class children of the same general age group and grade placement.[21] In comparing the average T-units of the Brownsville students, she found no significant difference: the Brownsville students produced 3,449 T-units that were used in the research, and the average length was 7.03 words[22] as opposed to the 7.97 words of the white, middle-class first graders in the O'Donnell, Griffin, and Norris study.[23] Levy also discovered that the Brownsville first graders used a total number of words ranging from 631 to 3,956 (with a mean of 1,524) and that the number of different words that they used ranged from 187 to 533 (mean 336). From these data, she concluded "that none of the children can reasonably be described as non-verbal."[24]

The following are the most important conclusions in the Levy study for teachers of reading at the primary level: "The findings here indicated that, insofar as oral language knowledge is related to learning reading, the population represented by the subjects has adequate language skills. There was no evidence that the children are too deficient in linguistic abilities to learn to decode words and comprehend written communication."[25]

Every child entering primary school does so with a well-developed background in language and in linguistic structures, and it is on this background that effective instructional strategies can and must be modeled. Teachers who know how to make the most of their students' backgrounds will begin to be more aware of student abilities rather than of student deficits, and the entire learning process will thus be facilitated.

Teacher Attitudes Toward Dialect Speakers

The attitudes of teachers toward their students, particularly in the early grades, have long been thought to be influential in the development of students as people. Recent research appears to substantiate the fact that the attitudes of teachers are all-important in instructional situations. An attitude of acceptance and caring on the part of teachers toward students or toward things that students do helps to promote an atmosphre conducive to learning. This is a most significant point for teachers to remember, especially in early learning encounters where young children may take personally the correction of a mispronounced word or of some untoward behavior.

It is important initially for teachers to let students know, "I like you and respect you as a person. If I seek to correct something that you are doing, this does not change my feeling for you. I hope that you like and respect me as a person. But if I say today is Tuesday and you are sure that it is Wednesday, I hope that you will correct me. This will not mean that you like me or respect me any less, will it?"

Laray Brown points out that "If the teacher is concerned only with the 'correctness' of the child's speech and not his perceptions, and attempts to force him into a system not his own (negating his system all the time), the child becomes alienated from the teacher and the culture the teacher represents."[26]

The Simons/Johnson study reaches a similar conclusion: "...the authors' observations in many urban schools and their work with teachers of Black dialect speaking children suggests that the teachers' handling of dialect during reading instruction is a very important factor in Black children's poor reading performance."[27]

Teachers cannot always foresee the impact that some of their actions may have upon impressionable youngsters, particularly in the very early grades. Annabel Bixby recently surveyed eighteen students who had been her kindergarten students twenty years ago. Most spoke favorably of their kindergarten experience, devoid as it was of formality and competition for grades. However, she reports, "Many described incidents that occurred in primary grades that probably seemed trivial to their teachers but to these students seemed important. Some described times when teachers either hurt their feelings, humiliated them in front of classmates, or were unfair to them—small incidents that loomed large in their memories. *Negative experiences with teachers were mostly vividly recalled and described from their early school years, while few reported such experiences in later school life.*"[28]

If learning takes place optimally in supportive environments, as most research seems to indicate that it does, then it is professionally incumbent upon primary teachers to provide each and every student the kind of support which will motivate and enhance learning. The "off-switch" can easily be activated in these early years, particularly if the child's use of language becomes the constant target of correction and, in his/her eyes, perhaps ridicule.

Teachers need to realize that just as they affect students, students affect them. All teaching involves interaction, and mature teachers will attempt to analyze their own reactions intelligently and fairly. Schlechty and Atwood write, "...the quality and quantity of teacher interaction seem to be influenced by such factors as student sex, teacher perceptions of student achievement, and even a student's physical location in the classroom."[29] Some teachers may be unaware that factors of this kind enter into classroom interaction. Knowledge and awareness of such reactions can lead to improved teacher/student relations.

It is most important for teachers to have a realistic view of their own tolerances or thresholds and to work at expanding these tolerance or thresholds as they mature in the profession. For example, some teachers are possessive of their space and do not like to have it intruded upon. Such teachers may make subconscious judgments about students who have a different space concept, students who like to be physically close and to touch. A judgment based on this sort of reaction is usually masked: "Johnny can't sit still" or "Susie can't seem to follow directions." Many experienced teachers cannot admit to themselves why they react to some students as they do.

Labov notes, "The essential fallacy of the verbal-deprivation theory lies in tracing the educational failure of the child to his personal deficiencies. At present, these deficiencies are said to be caused by his home environment. It is traditional to explain a child's failure in school by *his* inadequacy; but when failure reaches such massive proportions, it seems necessary to look at the social and cultural obstacles to learning and the inability of the school to adjust to the social situation."[30]

Jane Torrey addresses primary school teachers particularly in saying, "Children in the lower grades commonly accept a teacher as a kind of substitute mother. Teachers make use of this attitude in motivating and teaching. However, no such mother-child relationship can be established with someone who cannot accept the other person and his ways as legitimate."[31] Her contentions are particularly compelling in the light of a recent research study which reviewed the characteristic traits of Black children who are achievers. Among the generalizations which this fascinating research report reaches is that "Black achievers, for the most part, come from families whose occupational level might be categorized as upper-lower class and above."[32] The study, not surprisingly in light of the findings of Labov's studies,[33] "indicates that the majority of Black academic achievers are female." But most important for teachers to remember is the fact that "While it is generally noted that *there is little difference between the males and females in intelligence,* girls have been found to be identified as gifted at a 2:1 ratio."[34]

Perhaps the most surprising finding in the Shade research is that "one of the most baffling characteristics of black achievers is their apparent ability to induce negative reactions from their teachers." Shade continues, "Although black girls seem to obtain a more favorable response from teachers than do black males, in general black achievers, regardless of sex, are found to be objects of rejection by teachers." And then Shade specifies the bases of her conclusions: "Black gifted achievers were found to receive less attention, to be least praised, and to be most criticized in a classroom—even when compared to their nonachieving and nongifted black counterparts,"[35] which says volumes about Black stereotyping.

Shade contends, "Black students respond best to teachers who are warm, interested, child-oriented, and have high expectations of students."[36] Nearly everything written about the education of Black students would support this statement. Anastasiow and Hanes, for example, write, "Our position is that the cultural variables in the poverty child's ability to learn to read are his intelligence, his ability to comprehend language as it is spoken in school, *and the teacher's acceptance of the child's dialect.*"[37] The acceptance of a child's dialect and the acceptance of that child are very closely akin in the early grades—at least in the mind of the child.

In his report of 1966, Coleman felt that better physical plants and better materials are not the answer to the learning problems of minority students nearly so much as good teachers are.[38] What Coleman suggests calls for greater objective self-assessment and sufficient education in dialectology and in the sociology of race and culture to dispel many of the attitudinal barriers which may affect the learning of dialect-speaking minority students.

A Beginning for Teachers

Most teachers wish to be effective. Many simply do not know what steps to take initially to help them deal with students who are very much different from themselves. The following steps may help teachers who wish to deal more effectively and productively with students who come from backgrounds different from theirs.[39]

1. Learn as much as you can about the dialect(s) your students speak. [See the list of some characteristics of Black English which appears earlier in this chapter, pp. 66-67.]

2. Respect your students' dialects and their right to use them.

3. Learn to differentiate between a real error in oral reading and a translation from what is written to the dialect of the reader.

4. Respect *what* your students say and write for the ideas contained in their statements.

5. Avoid making judgments about students' intellect based largely upon *how* they express themselves.

6. Let your language be a model for your students without allowing it to be a wall which separates you from them.

7. Work to expand your students' language bases by having them listen to records or view films which represent a variety of language situations.

8. Work to expand your students' experiential bases by exposing them to the community and by bringing into the classroom local citizens from various walks of life.

9. Demonstrate to your students that you value them and are as willing to learn from them as you hope they are to learn from you.

Chapter 9
THE PAST AND THE FUTURE OF READING

The present of reading is so much with us that it is easy to forget its past and to ignore its future. The onset of the ascendancy of reading in the western world occurred when Johann Gutenberg invented a printing press using movable type, probably in Strasbourg in either 1436 or 1437. It took some two decades before Gutenberg produced his first book from this press, the exquisite Mazarin Bible, also known as the Gutenberg Bible, whose publication date is thought to be 1456.

Gutenberg did not experience instant fame and fortune as a result of his first major publication. Indeed, Johann Fust, a goldsmith from whom Gutenberg had borrowed the money to set up his press and produce his Bible, foreclosed when the printer was unable to repay his loan, and the press fell into the hands of Fust and his son-in-law, Peter Schoffer, who continued to operate it.

It was not until 1471-72 that William Caxton learned the art of printing with movable type in Cologne. In Bruges three years afterwards, in 1475, with the help of Colard Mansion, Caxton printed *The Recuyell of the Historyes of Troye,* the first book ever to be printed in English. The following year, close by Westminster, Caxton set up a press which, before the turn of the century, had produced editions of approximately one hundred books.

This is not to suggest that suddenly reading became a favorite pastime of the British peasantry. Indeed, few people in European or British society were able to read; books were therefore produced largely for the educated few, mostly clergymen, who were literate.

It was really not until the Reformation, which began some sixty-odd years after the publication of the Mazarin Bible, that Martin Luther espoused the doctrine that every person should be able to read sufficiently well to be able to read Scripture, thereby making every person an interpreter of Holy Writ.

Gutenberg and Luther were instrumentalities in the ascendancy of reading. One provided the physical means of producing books in multiple copies; the other provided a philosophical basis for encouraging the masses to learn how to read. Two major stumbling blocks to universal reading literacy were overcome in less than a century, but literacy did not begin to sweep Europe or Britain as a result.

Shakespeare and Marlowe and Kyd were writing during this period, but they were not writing to be read. Rather, they were writing to be performed and their audiences were largely illiterate. Indeed, playwrights of the day went to extraordinary lengths to see that written versions of their plays did not leave the theatre after rehearsals because they feared that their material would be pirated were it to get into the wrong hands. Popular literature remained essentially part of the oral tradition which developed in the story-telling and history-preserving traditions of ancient peoples throughout the world. Literature that was intended to be read remained essentially a literature produced by clerics for a clerical audience. Other literate people in this society consisted of some merchants who had sufficient reading and writing ability to enable them to keep records of their transactions, even as the tradespeople of ancient Sumeria, Babylonia, and Egypt had before them.

The historical purpose of writing is essentially fourfold: (1) preserves tradition, (2) it allows expression, (3) it records information, and (4) it makes possible the dissemination of that information. The ancient drawings in the caves at Altamira and Lascaux, the carefully wrought Coptic inscriptions found in the Egyptian pyramids, the cuneiform wedges found on ancient tablets of clay, the graffiti found on the sides of Pompeian buildings or on the walls of the New York subway system—all these examples of writing and recording serve such purposes.

As long as society was essentially agrarian, there was very little need for the average person to be able to read. An economy based largely on the exchange of products is a much less abstract economy than one which is based, to a large extent, on the exchange of information. When the exchange of products is a simple one-to-one exchange, such as one person's trading a sheep that has been raised for a garment produced by a neighbor, no written records need enter into the transfer. When entrepreneurs are involved, as they necessarily are if exchanges take place among people who are too geographically distant from each other to deal on a one-to-one basis, written records become a necessity, and some form of literacy becomes a requirement for the entrepreneurs. When an economy comes to be based on services as much as or more than on goods, as is the case with our present economy, then literacy is a requirement for anyone who wishes to participate fully in that economy and in the society.

It is the coming of the Industrial Age that really marked a turning point in the importance of reading. On the one hand, an industrialized society becomes sufficiently complex that information must be systematically created and preserved; and on the other hand, such a society requires continually higher levels of education for its members, making it incumbent upon them to know how to read in order to have available to them the information which they are required to master.

If we view reading as part of a continuum stretching back to the earliest human history on earth, we find that it does not soon appear on that continuum in any way. Humans and human-like creatures used language in some systematic form for eons before they transmitted it into writing; and then they wrote pictographically, so that communication was through pictures rather than through abstract symbols.

The move from pictographic representation to ideographic representation was an incomprehensibly enormous advance for the species to make, because it took humankind to a totally new level of abstract representation. And the leap from ideographic writing to alphabetic writing probably represents an advance more significant and more incredible than that of putting the first humans on the moon.

Edward T. Hall speaks to the development of writing and, by extension, of its concomitant, reading:

> The history of art is almost three times longer than that of writing, and the relationship between the two types of expression can be seen in the earliest forms of writing, such as the Egyptian hieroglyphics. However, very few people treat art as a system of communication which is historically linked with language.[1]

The oldest written records left by humankind are drawings etched on the walls of caves or carved on the materials from which their simple tools were made. In the time that such graphic representations were made, everyone within that culture could read them; that is, they could look at them and know what they meant. The level of abstraction required in order for a person to read them was much lower than the level of abstraction required of one who is trying to learn to read an alphabetic language today, and teachers must understand this difference. Getting messages from pictures in a book *is* a form of reading. Seeing pictographic highway signs indicating crossings or bicycle routes and being able to interpret them *is* a form of reading, and most people can handle such reading. Indeed, on our time continuum, the first, very small dot represents just such reading. The dot grows slightly larger as pictographic and alphabetic writing develop, but it is still so small as to be almost imperceptible, And it remains imperceptibly small on up through the invention of the printing press and the urgings toward literacy of Martin Luther.

Only in the last seventy-five years has reading begun to appear on the continuum as a large circle rather than as a dot. Its appearance as a large circle has been coincident with the enormous growth, on the one hand, of industry and, on the other hand, of free, public education which is made available through legal mandate in most developed areas of the world and which is imposed upon young people through compulsory attendance laws in most places. Because this is the current situation, many people tend to forget the past and fail to recognize that in the future the continuum may place reading in a much less important position relatively speaking than it is in today.

This is not to suggest that reading will fall into a position of unimportance or that human beings in the future will not have to be able to read. Reading is firmly entrenched as a requisite skill which members of complex societies must possess. However, other means of communication, many of them invented or refined and made readily available to millions of people within the past century, may drastically alter the purposes to which people turn their reading skill.

In addition, significant strides are being made in reading instruction. For example, one of the most promising systems which has been developed is tightly organized and highly sequential; it aims to teach the skills of literacy—reading and writing—as early and as quickly as possible. While it is still too early to generalize on the results of a system such as this, it is encouraging to find that some school districts which have employed it have eliminated illiteracy in all students by fifth grade.

As teaching systems of this sort are developed, universal literacy may be achieved. There will one day be no illiterates in developed nations, and other elements of communications systems will occupy a more important position on the continuum than reading does. Such areas as subliminal communication, which is already being studied seriously by a number of eminent scholars and researchers, may be developed in ways that will enable people to communicate by means which seem unavailable to them today.

For the present, initial reading instruction is vital and necessary. It is most likely to be successful if those teaching it are not overburdened with large classes and if they are continuingly aware of scientific developments in the broad area of human communication. In most cases this means that school districts should be spending much more money than they now do on the staffing of the primary grades, on providing materials for these grades, and on providing teachers at the primary level with ample opportunity to continue their educations so that they can be current in their teaching techniques. Money thus spent will substantially reduce expenditures for remedial instruction in reading later on when, for the most part, it is offered too late to do much good.

But broader benefits will accrue to society if all children learn to read in the primary grades—and this *can* happen. Of greatest importance is the fact that in developed societies, literate people have a greater sense of their own worth than those who are not literate. On the crassest of levels, literate people contribute more to society in tax revenues than illiterates do. Their other contributions generally are also such that society benefits from their ability to exercise their literacy.

It is necessary to realize that for better or worse, civilization is moving conceptually at a breakneck speed. Writing of the past, Alvin Toffler states, "In stagnant societies, the past crept forward into the present and repeated itself in the future. In such a society, the most sensible way to prepare a child was to arm him with the skills of the past—for these were precisely the same skills he would need in the future."[2] To a large extent, this was the form that education took until the beginning of this century. Future orientation is a relatively new phenomenon. While Toffler recognizes that such basics as reading and writing and mathematics will be necessary to people who wish to function well in the society of the future, he cautions his readers that "... millions of children today are forced by law to spend precious hours of their lives grinding away at materials whose future utility is highly questionable."[3] His most telling message for reading teachers is that "Tomorrow's illiterate will not be the man who can't read; he will be the man who has not learned how to learn."[4]

What Toffler really means is that reading is an instrumentality. Being able to read does not *make* a person smart or productive or successful. Rather, being able to read makes it more possible for a person to function intelligently and effectively within modern society. This is the perspective that reading teachers most need to develop. In this spirit the writer presents this book to his readers.

FOOTNOTES AND REFERENCES

Chapter 1. A Perspective on Reading Instruction, pp. 15-19.

[1]New York: McGraw-Hill Book Co., 1976.

[2]Lake Forest, Ill.: National School Public Relations Association, 1955, p. 5.

[3]New York: Holt.

[4]*Elementary English Review* 19 (April and May 1942): 125-30 and 183-86.

[5]"The Story of the Bloomfield System," in Leonard Bloomfield and Clarence L. Barnhart, *Let's Read: A Linguistic Approach* (Detroit: Wayne State University Press, 1961), p. 9.

[6]*Ibid.*

[7]"Teaching Children to Read," in Bloomfield and Barnhart, *Let's Read,* p. 26.

[8]Charles C. Fries, *Linguistics and Reading* (New York: Holt, Rinehart and Winston, 1963) p. 131.

[9]*Ibid.,* p. 130. Fries's italics.

[10]*Ibid.,* p. 131. Italics added.

[11]*Loc. cit.,* p. xvii.

[12]George A. Miller, "Some Preliminaries to Psycholinguistics," *American Psychologist 20* (1965): 18.

[13]*Teaching Elementary Reading,* 2d ed. (New York: Appleton-Century-Crofts, 1962), p. 378.

[14]William S. Gray. *The Teaching of Reading and Writing,* Monographs on Fundamental Education 10 (Paris: UNESCO, 1956): 68.

[15]Edited by Jeanne Chall, vol. 77, part 2 (Chicago: National Society for the Study of Education, 1978).

[16]San Francisco: W. H. Freeman, 1973.

[17]San Francisco: W. H. Freeman, 1973.

[18]New York: Vintage Books, 1960.

[19]Reading, Mass.: Addison-Wesley, 1974.

[20]New York: William Morrow and Co., 1974.

[21]Reading, Mass.: Addison-Wesley, 1976.

Chapter 2. The Learning Processes of Young Children, pp. 20-28.

[1] Frances L. Ilg, "The Child from Three to Eight with Implications for Reading," an address presented at a conference on *Teaching the Young Child to Read,* Washington, D.C., November 14-16, 1962, and reproduced in some detail in Nila Banton Smith, *Reading Instruction for Today's Children* (Englewood Cliffs, N.J.: Prentice-Hall, 1963), p. 26.

[2]*Ibid.,* p. 27. Ilg's italics.

[3]*Ibid.*

[4]Herman T. Epstein, "Growth Spurts during Brain Development: Implications for Educational Policy and Practice," in Jeanne S. Chall and Allan F. Mirsky, eds., *Education and the Brain,* 77th Yearbook of the National Society for the Study of Education, Part II (Chicago: National Society for the Study of Education, 1978), p. 344.

[5]R.S. Hampleman, "A Study of the Comparative Reading Achievement of Early and Late School Starters," *Elementary English* 34 (1959): 331-34.

[6]L. B. Carter, "The Effect of Early School Entrance on the Scholastic Achievement of Elementary School Children in the Austin Public Schools," *Journal of Educational Research* 50 (1956): 91-113.

[7]Albert J. Harris, *How to Increase Your Reading Ability,* 4th ed. (New York: Longmans, Green and Co., 1961).

[8]E. L. Thorndike, *The Psychology of Learning* (New York: Teachers College, Columbia University, 1923).

[9]Arnold Gesell, *The Mental Growth of the Pre-School Child* (New York: Macmillan Co., 1925). See also his later books, *Infancy and Human Growth* (New York: Macmillan Co., 1928) and *The First Five Years of Life* (New York: Harper and Bros., 1940).

[10]See Dolores Durkin, "Children Who Read before Grade One," *Reading Teacher* 14 (1961): 163-66, as well as her *Children Who Read Early* (New York: Teachers College Press, Columbia University, 1966).

[11]Cambridge, Mass.: Harvard University Press, 1960, p. 33.

[12]Lawrence Kohlberg, "Early Education: A Cognitive-Development View" (unpublished paper, University of Chicago, n. d.), cited in Dolores Durkin, "When Should Children Begin to Read?" in Helen M. Robinson, ed., *Innovation and Change in Reading Instruction,* 67th Yearbook of the National Society for the Study of Education, Part II (Chicago: National Society for the Study of Education, 1968), p. 67.

[13]Jeanne S. Chall and Allan F. Mirsky, "The Implications of Education," in *Education and the Brain,* p. 371.

[14]Robert M. Gagné, "Some New Views of Learning and Instruction," *Phi Delta Kappan* 51 (1970): 469.

[15]See particularly Bruner's *The Process of Education,* aforementioned, and his *On Knowing: Essays for the Left Hand* (New York: Atheneum House, 1966).

[16]See particularly *Taxonomy of Educational Objectives, Handbook I* (New York: David McKay Co., 1956), which Bloom edited.

[17]David H. Russell, "Research on the Processes of Thinking with Some Applications to Reading," *Elementary English* 42 (April 1965): 378.

[18]Jean Piaget and Barbel Inhelder, *The Psychology of the Child* (New York: Basic Books, 1969), p. 6.

[19]Madeline Hunter, "The Learning Process," in Dwight Allen and Eli Seifman, eds., *The Teacher's Handbook* (Glenview, Ill.: Scott, Foresman and Co., 1971), p. 158. Italics omitted.

[20]*Ibid.,* p. 159. Italics omitted.

[21]*Ibid.,* p. 160.

[22]Albert North Whitehead, "The Rhythm of Education," Chapter II in *The Aims of Education* (New York: Macmillan Co., 1959), p. 24. This essay was first published as a pamphlet (London: Christopher's, 1922).

[23]*Ibid.,* p. 25.

[24]Ibid., *p. 26.*

[25]*Ibid.,* p. 27.

[26]Epstein, "Growth Spurts," p. 343.

[27]*Ibid.*, pp. 343-44. Epstein's italics.

[28]*Ibid.*, p. 350.

[29]*Ibid.*, p. 344.

[30]Kohlberg, "Early Education," p. 67.

[31]For a clear discussion of hemisphericity see Betty Jane Wagner, "Educational Drama and the Brain's Right Hemisphere," in R. Baird Shuman, ed., *Educational Drama for Today's Schools* (Metuchen, N.J.: Scarecrow Press, 1978), pp. 133-54. Jerome Bruner's *On Knowing: Essays for the Left Hand,* aforementioned, is concerned with this central topic. Also of considerable value to teachers is Bob Samples's *The Metaphoric Mind* (Reading, Mass.: Addison-Wesley, 1976). A more specialized book on the topic is Robert Ornstein's *The Psychology of Consciousness* (New York: Viking, 1972).

[32]As reported by Merlin C. Wittrock, "Education and the Cognitive Processes of the Brain," in *Education and the Brain,* aforementioned, *pp. 66-67.*

[33]Wittrock, "Cognitive Processes," p. 74.

[34]Wittrock cites numerous studies, among them Michael R. Raugh and Richard C. Atkinson, "A Mnemonic Method for Learning a Second-language Vocabulary," *Journal of Educational Psychology* 67 (1975): 1-16; Joel R. Levin, "What Have We Learned About Maximizing What Children Learn?" in Joel R. Levin and Vernon L. Allen, eds., *Cognitive Learning in Children: Theories and Strategies* (New York: Academic Press, 1976), pp. 105-34; and William D. Rohwer, Jr., "Images and Pictures in Children's Learning: Research Results and Instructional Implications," *Psychological Bulletin* 73 (1970): 393-403.

[35]Wittrock, "Cognitive Processes," p. 97. The study to which he refers is Carolyn B. Marks, Marleen J. Doctorow, and Merlin C. Wittrock, "Word Frequency and Reading Comprehension," *Journal of Educational Research* 67 (1974): 259-62.

Chapter 3. Reading Readiness, pp. 29-34.

[1]"Readiness Is Being," *Childhood Education* 38 (November 1961): 116.

[2]David P. Ausubel, *The Psychology of Meaningful Verbal Learning* (New York: Grune and Stratton, 1963), p. 33.

[3]Albert J. Harris, "Child Development and Reading," in Marion D. Jenkinson, ed., *Reading Instruction: An International Forum* (Newark, Del.: International Reading Association, 1967), pp. 336-49, *passim.*

[4]Ausubel, *Psychology,* p. 111.

[5]*Ibid.*

[6]Edward W. Dolch, *Teaching Primary Reading,* 3d ed. (Champaign, Ill.: Garrard Press, 1960), pp. 45-66, *passim.*

[7]Dolores Durkin, "What Does Research Say About the Time to Begin Reading Instruction?" *Journal of Educational Research* 64 (October 1970): 52.

[8]*Ibid.*

[9]Ausubel, *Psychology,* p. 32.

[10]Miles A. Tinker and Constance M. McCullough, *Teaching Elementary Reading,* 2d ed. (New York: Appleton-Century-Crofts, 1962), p. 54.

[11]Michael A. and Lise Wallach, *Teaching All Children to Read* (Chicago: University of Chicago Press, 1976), p. 72.

82

[12]Dolores Durkin, "An Earlier Start in Reading?" *Elementary School Journal* 43 (December 1962): 151.

[13]Boston: Houghton Mifflin Co., 1936.

[14]By Arthur I. Gates, G. L. Bond, and D. H. Russell (New York: Bureau of Publications, Teachers College, Columbia University, 1939).

[15]Mabel V. Morphett and Carleton Washburne, "When Should Children Begin to Read?" *Elementary School Journal* 31 (March 1931): 496-508.

[16]See for example R. Rosenthal and L. Jacobson, *Pygmalion in the Classroom: Teacher Expectation and Pupils' Intellectual Development* (New York: Holt, Rinehart and Winston, 1968) or Rosenthal's "Self-Fulfilling Prophecies in the Classroom: Teachers' Expectations as Unintended Determinants of Pupils' Intellectual Competence," in M. Deutsch, I. Katz, and A. R. Jensen, eds., *Social Class, Race, and Psychological Development* (New York: Holt, Rinehart and Winston, 1968).

[17]Durkin, "What Does Research Say," p. 56.

[18]Jack A. Holmes, "What Should and Could Johnny Learn to Read?" in J. Allen Figurel, ed., *Challenge and Experiment in Reading* (Newark, Del.: International Reading Association, 1962), p. 240-41.

[19]F. L. Ilg and L. B. Ames, *School Readiness: Behavior Tests Used at Gesell Institute* (New York: Harper and Row, 1965).

[20]Jeannette Jansky and Katrina de Hirsch, *Preventing Reading Failure: Prediction, Diagnosis, Intervention* (New York: Harper and Row, 1972), p. 4.

[21]The citation is to J. M. Tanner, *Education and Physical Growth* (London: University of London Press, 1961).

[22]Albert J. Harris, "Evaluating Reading Readiness Tests," in Coleman Morrison, ed., *Problem Areas in Reading—Some Observations and Recommendations,* Rhode Island College Reading Conference Proceedings (Providence, R. I.: Oxford Press, 1965), pp. 11-12.

[23]Clarence S. Darrow, *Farmington* (Chicago: A. C. McClurg and Co., 1904), pp. 40-41.

[24]Norbert Weiner, *Ex-Prodigy* (Cambridge, Mass.: Massachusetts Institute of Technology Press, 1964), p. 62.

[25]Durkin, "An Earlier Start," p. 151.

[26]George D. Spache et al., *A Study of a Longitudinal First-Grade Readiness Program,* Cooperative Research Project No. 2742 (Tallahassee, Fla.: Florida State Department of Education, 1965).

Chapter 4. The Basal Reader Approach, pp. 35-40.

[1]Nila Banton Smith, *Reading Instruction for Today's Children* (Englewood Cliffs, N.J.: Prentice-Hall, 1963), p. 99.

[2]These two unpublished reports are cited by Miles A. Tinker and Constance M. McCullough in *Teaching Elementary Reading,* 2d ed. (New York: Appleton-Century-Crofts, 1962), p. 293.

[3]Douglas P. Barnard and James DeGracie, "Vocabulary Analysis of New Primary Reading Series," *Reading Teacher* 30 (November 1976): 179.

[4]Leo V. Rodenborn and Earlene Washburn, "Some Implications of the New Basal Readers," *Elementary English* 51 (September 1974): 886.

[4a]*Ibid.*

[5]For convincing evidence of the need for the individualization of reading instruction at this stage in a child's development, see Jack A. Holmes, "When Should and Could Johnny Learn to Read?" in J. Allen Figurel, ed., *Challenge and Experiment in Reading* (Newark, Del.: International Reading Association Proceedings, 1962), pp. 237-41.

[6]As presented by Lyman G. Hunt, Jr., the con challenger in Ralph C. Staiger's "Basal Reading Programs: How Do They Stand Today?" in Nila Banton Smith, ed., *Current Issues in Reading* (Newark, Del.: International Reading Association, 1969), p. 303.

[7]*Ibid.*, p. 305.

[8]Arthur V. Olson, "An Analysis of the Vocabulary of Seven Primary Reading Series," *Elementary English* 43 (March 1965): 26164.

[9]Barnard and DeGracie, "Vocabulary Analysis," pp. 178-79.

[10]George D. and Evelyn B. Spache, *Reading in the Elementary School* (Boston: Allyn and Bacon, 1969), pp. 77-89, *passim.*

[11]Rodenborn and Washburn, "Some Implications," p. 886.

[12]Barnard and DeGracie, "Vocabulary Analysis," p. 178.

[13]Rodenborn and Washburn, "Some Implications," p. 888.

[14]Fred Busch, "Basals Are Not for Reading," *Teaching College Record* 72 (September 1970): 30.

[15]Terry D. Johnson, *Reading: Teaching and Learning* (New York: Macmillan Co., 1973), pp. 22-23.

[16]Thomas R. Schnell and Judith Sweeney, "Sex Role Bias in Basal Readers," *Elementary English* 52 (May 1975): 738.

[17]"Images of Males and Females in Elementary School Textbooks in Five Subject Areas," in *Sex Role Stereotyping in the Schools,* rev. ed. (Washington, D.C.: National Education Association, 1977), pp. 57-67.

[18]See Erik Erikson, "Identity and the Life Cycle," *Psychological Issues* 1 (1959): 82-88.

Chapter 5. Phonics, pp. 41-47.

[1]Paul McKee, *Reading: A Program for the Elementary School* (Boston: Houghton Mifflin, Co., 1966), p. 74. Some reading experts include more letters than these as regular. Dechant (see footnote 2) includes *y* (as a consonant) and *z*. Edward B. Fry, *Elementary Reading Instruction* (New York: McGraw-Hill Book Co., 1977), p. 24, includes, along with *y* and *z, s* (as in *sit*), *c* (as in *cat*), and *g* (as in *get*). I omit *y* because it is generally a vowel, *z* because it represents two sounds (*zebra, azure*), *s* because it represents the /s/ sound (*sit*) and /z/ (*its*), *c* because it represents the hard sound (*cat*) as well as the soft sound (*certain*), and *g* which can be hard (*gun*) or soft *(gem).*

[2]Emerald Dechant, *Linguistics, Phonics and the Teaching of Reading* (Springfield, Ill.: Charles C. Thomas, 1969), p. 36.

[3]*Ibid.*

[4]Albert J. Mazurkiewicz, *Teaching about Phonics* (New York: St. Martin's Press, 1976), p. 32.

[5]See Gertrude Hildreth, *Teaching Reading* (New York: Holt, Rinehart and Winston, 1958); see also her "Some Misconceptions Concerning Phonics," *Elementary English* 36 (January 1957): 26-27.

[6]Betty Berdiansky, Bruce Cronnell, and John Koehler, *Spelling-Sound Relations and Primary Form-Class Descriptions for Speech-Comprehension Vocabularies of 6-9 Year Olds,* Technical Report No. 15 (Los Alamitos, Calif.: Southwest Regional Laboratory for Educational Research and Development, 1968).

[7]For a fuller discussion of this matter see Albert J. Mazurkiewicz, *Teaching,* pp. 31-32.

[8]*Ibid.,* pp. 69-71 and 32-33.

[9]Jack Bagford, "The Role of Phonics in Teaching Reading," in J. Allen Figurel, ed., *Reading and Realism* (Newark, Del.: International Reading Association, 1967), p. 83.

[10]*Ibid.,* p. 85

[11]Franklin set forth his system in his *Scheme for a New Alphabet and Reformed Mode of Spelling* which was published in Philadelphia in 1768.

[12]Edward B. Fry, *Elementary Reading,* p. 72.

[13]Emery P. Bleismer and Betty H. Yarborough, "A Comparison of Ten Different Beginning Reading Programs in First Grade," *Phi Delta Kappan* 56 (June 1965): 500-504.

[14]Jeanne S. Chall, *Learning to Read: The Great Debate* (New York: McGraw-Hill Book Co., 1967), p. 134. Professor Chall refers to chapter 3, "Research on Beginning Reading—Science or Ideology?"

[15]Ibid., p. 125.

[16]*Ibid.,* p. 307.

[17]William H. McGuffey, ed., *McGuffey's First Eclectic Reader,* rev. ed. (Cincinnati, Ohio: Van Antwerp, Bragg, and Co., 1879), p. ii.

[18]Mazurkiewicz, *Teaching, p. 132.*

Chapter 6. Linguistic Science and Reading Instruction, pp. 48-55.

[1]Charles C. Fries, *Linguistics and Reading* (New York: Holt, Rinehart and Winston, 1963), p. 36.

[2]Frank Smith, *Psycholinguistics and Reading* (New York: Holt, Rinehart and Winston, 1973), p. 1.

[3]Clarence L. Barnhart, "The Story of the Bloomfield System," in Leonard Bloomfield and Clarence L. Barnhart, *Let's Read: A Linguistic Approach* (Detroit: Wayne State University Press, 1961), p. 9.

[4]Dolores Durkin, *Phonics, Linguistics, and Reading* (New York: Teachers College, Columbia University, 1972), p. 13.

[5]The first example avoids the redundancy of the second in which *three* clearly indicates plurality and -*s* merely reiterates it.

[6]Charlton Laird, *The Miracle of Language* (New York: Premier Books, 1953), p. 159. Laird's italics.

[7]Leonard Bloomfield, "Linguistics and Reading," *Elementary English Review* 19 (April 1942): 125.

[8]Leonard Bloomfield, "Teaching Children to Read," in Bloomfield and Barnhart, *Let's Read,* p. 24. Bloomfield's italics.

[9]J. N. Hook, "Spelling: Trial and Terror," in *The Teaching of High School English* (New York: Ronald Press, 1972), p. 417. See also Dolores Durkin, *Phonics,* p. 2.

[10]Bloomfield, *Let's Read,* p. 32. Bloomfield's italics.

11Ronald Wardhaugh, "Is the Linguistic Approach an Improvement in Reading Instruction?" in Nila Banton Smith, ed., *Current Issues in Reading* (Newark, Del.: International Reading Association, 1969), p. 256.

12Charles C. Fries, *Linguistics*, p. 96. Fries's italics.

13*Ibid.*, p. 94. Fries's italics.

14*Ibid.*, p. 100. Fries's italics.

15*The Teaching of Reading: A Second Report, Part I of The Thirty-sixth Yearbook of the National Society for the Study of Education* (Bloomington, Ill.: Public School Publishing Co., 1937), pp. 25-28.

16*Linguistics*, p. 120. Fries's italics.

17*Ibid.*, p. 121. Fries's italics.

18*Ibid.*, p. 156.

19Kenneth Goodman in Nila Banton Smith, ed., *Current Issues in Reading, p. 269.*

Chapter 7. Miscue Analysis, pp. 56-64.

1Portions of this chapter appeared as Chapter 6, "Miscue Analysis as a Key to Understanding Reading Problems," in R. Baird Shuman, *Strategies in Teaching Reading: Secondary* (Washington, D.C.: National Education Association, 1978), pp. 54-61. Copyright © 1978 by the National Education Association of the United States. Used with permission.

1a Noam Chomsky, *Syntactic Structures* (The Hague: Mouton, 1957).

2Ronald Wardhaugh, "Is the Linguistic Approach an Improvement in Reading Instruction?" in Nila Banton Smith, ed., *Current Issues in Reading* (Newark, Del.: International Reading Association, 1969), p. 263.

3*Ibid.*

4*Ibid.*, p. 264.

4a Detroit: Wayne State University Press, 1967.

5Kenneth S. Goodman, "Analysis of Oral Reading Miscues: Applied Psycholinguistics," *Reading Research Quarterly* 5 (Fall 1969): 11.

6*Ibid.*

7*Ibid.*

8*Ibid.*, pp. 19-26.

9See Frank Smith, *Psycholinguistics and Reading* (New York: Holt, Rinehart, and Winston, 1973), p. 80.

10Kenneth S. Goodman, "Analysis."

11Carolyn L. Burke and Kenneth S. Goodman, "When a Child Reads: A Psycholinguistic Analysis," *Elementary English* 47 (January 1970): 121-29.

12Rose-Marie Weber, "The Study of Oral Reading Errors: A Survey of the Literature," *Reading Research Quarterly* 4 (1968): 96-119.

13Smith, *Psycholinguistics*, p. 80

14Kenneth S. Goodman, "A Linguistic Study of Cues and Miscues in Reading," *Elementary English* 42 (1965): 39-44.

15Goodman, "Analysis," p. 16.

86

16W. Nelson Francis, *The Structure of American English* (New York: Ronald Press, 1958), p. 556.

17Kenneth R. Johnson, "What Should Be Taught to Students Who Speak Black Dialect?" in R. Baird Shuman, ed., *Questions English Teachers Ask* (Rochelle Park, N.J.: Hayden Book Co., 1977), p. 172.

18*Ibid.*, pp. 172-73.

19William Labov, *The Study of Nonstandard English* (Champaign, Ill.: National Council of Teachers of English, 1970), p. 44. See also Marvin Cohn and Cynthia D'Alessandro, "When Is a Decoding Error Not a Decoding Error?" *Reading Teacher* 32 (December 1978): 341-44.

20Distributed by Vision Quest, Inc., 7715 North Sheridan Road, Chicago, IL 60626. For a fuller discussion of this see *Educational Drama for Today's Schools,* R. Baird Shuman, ed. (Metuchen, N.J.: Scarecrow Press, 1978), pp. 41-58.

21Goodman, "Analysis," p. 14.

22James Peter Tortelli, "Simplified Psycholinguistic Diagnosis," *Reading Teacher* 29 (April 1976): 637.

23Laray Brown, " 'Correctness' and Reading," *Reading Teacher* 28 (December 1974): 277.

24*Ibid.*, p. 278.

25Aaron Lipton, "Miscalling While Reading Aloud: A Point of View," *Reading Teacher* 25 (May 1972): 760. Lipton's italics.

26For a more complete description of this useful technique, see Tortelli, "Diagnosis," pp. 637-39.

27Kenneth Goodman, ed., *Miscue Analysis: Applications to Reading Instruction* (Urbana, Ill.: National Council of Teachers of English; ERIC Clearinghouse on Reading and Communication Skills, 1973). [ED 080 973]

28Yetta Goodman, "Using Children's Reading Miscues for New Teaching Strategies," *Reading Teacher* 23 (February 1970): 455.

Chapter 8. Dialects and Early Reading Instruction, pp. 65-74.

1See William Labov, "Academic Ignorance and Black Intelligence," *Atlantic Monthly 229 (June 1972): 65.*

2For additional information see Roger W. Shuy, "A Linguistic Background for Developing Beginning Reading Materials for Black Children," in Joan Baratz and Roger W. Shuy, ed., *Teaching Black Children to Read* (Washington, D.C.: Center for Applied Linguistics, 1969), pp. 128-29; J. L. Dillard, *Black English: Its History and Use in the United States* (New York: Random House, 1972), p. 281; and Kenneth R. Johnson, "What Should Be Taught to Students Who Speak Black Dialect?" in R. Baird Shuman, ed., *Questions English Teachers Ask* (Rochelle Park, N.J.: Hayden Book Co., 1977), p. 172.

3Judy Iris Schwartz, "An Investigation of Attitudes on the Use of Black Dialect Materials for Beginning Reading Instruction," *Research in the Teaching of English* 9 (1075): 201.

4J. Steptoe, Stevie (New York: Harper and Row, 1969).

5Education Study Center, *Friends, Old Tales,* and *Ollie* (Washington, D.C.: Education Study Center, 1970).

6Schwartz, "Investigation," p. 202.

7*Ibid.*, p. 207.

8*Ibid.*, pp. 206-7.

[9]*Ibid.*, p. 201.

[10]Dorothy S. Strickland and William A. Stewart, "The Use of Dialect Readers: A Dialogue," in Bernice E. Cullinan, ed., *Black Dialects and Reading* (Urbana, Ill.: ERIC Clearinghouse on Reading and Communication Skills, 1974), p. 147.

[11]*Ibid.*, p. 150.

[12]*Ibid.*, p. 147.

[13]*Ibid.*

[14]Jane Torrey, "Illiteracy in the Ghetto," *Harvard Educational Review* 40 (1970): 254. Italics added.

[15]*Ibid.*, pp. 253, 256. Italics added.

[16]Herbert D. Simons and Kenneth R. Johnson, "Black English Syntax and Reading Interference," *Research in the Teaching of English* 8 (1974): 353.

[17]Martin Deutsch, "The Disadvantaged Child and the Learning Process," in A. H. Passow, ed., *Education in Depressed Areas* (New York: Teachers College Press, Columbia University, 1963), pp. 163-80.

[18]S. Engelmann, "How to Construct Effective Language Programs for the Poverty Child," in F. Williams, ed., *Language and Poverty: Perspectives on a Theme* (Chicago: Markham, 1970), pp. 102-22.

[19]Christopher Clausen, "Schoolmarms, the Linguists, and the Language," *Midwest Quarterly* 19 (Spring 1978): 233.

[20]Beatrice K. Levy, "Is the Oral Language of Inner City Children Adequate for Beginning Reading Instruction?" *Research in the Teaching of English* 7 (1973): 52.

[21]See Roy C. O'Donnell, William J. Griffin, and Raymond G. Norris, *Syntax of Kindergarten and Elementary School Children: A Transformational Analysis* (Champaign, Ill.: National Council of Teachers of English, 1967), pp. 44-45.

[22]Levy, "Oral Language," pp. 56-57.

[23]O'Donnell, *et. al.*, *Syntax*, p. 45.

[24]Levy, "Oral Language," pp. 55-56.

[25]*Ibid.*, p. 59.

[26]Laray Brown, " 'Correctness' and Reading," *Reading Teacher* 28 (December 1974): 278.

[27]Simons and Johnson, "Black English Syntax," p. 357

[28]Annabel A. Bixby, "Do Teachers Make a Difference?" *Childhood Education* 54 (April/May 1978): 288. Italics added.

[29]Phillip C. Schlechty and Helen E. Atwood, "The Student-Teacher Relationship," *Theory Into Practice* 16 (October 1977): 286.

[30]Labov, "Academic Ignorance," p. 66. Italics added.

[31]Torrey, "Illiteracy," p. 258.

[32]Barbara J. Shade, "Social-Psychological Traits of Achieving Black Children," *Negro Educational Review* 29 (April 1978): 80.

[33]See particularly William Labov, *Language in the Inner City: Studies in Black English* (Philadelphia: University of Pennsylvania Press, 1972) and *The Study of Nonstandard English* (Urbana, Ill.: National Council of Teachers of English, 1970)

[34]Shade, "Social-Psychological Traits," p. 82. Italics added.

[35]*Ibid.*, p. 85.

[36]*Ibid.*

[37]Nicholas J. Anastasiow and Michael L. Hanes, *Language Patterns of Poverty Children* (Springfield, Ill.: Charles C. Thomas, 1976), p. 145. Italics added.

[38]James S. Coleman, *Equality of Educational Opportunity* (Washington, D.C.: Department of Health, Education, and Welfare, 1966). See also his *Power and the Structures of Society* (New York: Norton, 1973).

[39]This list is reprinted from *Strategies in Teaching Reading: Secondary* by R. Baird Shuman (Washington, D.C.: National Education Association, 1978), p. 53. Copyright © 1978 by the National Education Association of the United States. Used with permission.

Chapter 9.   The Past and the Future of Reading, pp. 75-78.

[1]Edward T. Hall, *The Hidden Dimension* (Garden City, N.Y.: Doubleday and Co., 1966), p. 81.

[2]Alvin Toffler, *Future Shock* (New York: Bantam Books, 1970), p. 399.

[3]*Ibid*., pp. 409-10.

[4]*Ibid*., p. 414.